COUNSELING
AND
DRAMA

PSYCHODRAMA À DEUX

Marvin G. Knittel Ed. D.

COUNSELING
AND
DRAMA

Library of Congress Control Number: 2009912530
ISBN: Hardcover   978-1-4415-7894-5
                  Softcover   978-1-4415-7893-8
                  ebook   978-1-4415-7897-6

This book was printed in the United States of America.

To order additional copies of this book, contact:
Xlibris Corporation
1-888-795-4274
www.Xlibris.com
Orders@Xlibris.com
71580

CONTENTS

Foreword 9

Preface 13

Acknowledgments 15

Chapter 1   PSYCHODRAMA 17
Chapter 2   PSYCHODRAMA AND OTHER METHODS 19
Chapter 3   PSYCHODRAMA À DEUX 27
Chapter 4   SEARCH FOR MEANING 32
Chapter 5   SEXUAL ABUSE 36
Chapter 6   UNFINISHED BUSINESS 47
Chapter 7   DEPRESSION 50
Chapter 8   HANGING ON AND LETTING GO 59
Chapter 9   DEPENDENCY 66
Chapter 10   FAMILY COUNSELING 74
Chapter 11   AGING 83
Chapter 12   UNRESOLVED GUILT 87
Chapter 13   CONCLUSIONS 94

ABOUT THE AUTHOR

Marvin G. Knittel, Ed. D., is professor emeritus of counselor education at the University of Nebraska-Kearney, where for thirty-six years he alternately served as professor, chairman of the Department of Counseling and Educational Psychology, interim president, dean of instruction, academic vice president. He returned to the classroom for his final ten years at the university. He currently lives in Tucson, Arizona, where he devotes time to writing and volunteering.

His passion for psychodrama was born in a psychodrama workshop presented by Zerka Moreno at the Menninger Clinic in Topeka, Kansas. He continued his training under Dr. John Nolte, head of the National Psychodrama Training Center. During his thirty-six years with the university, Dr. Knittel taught psychodrama classes to graduate students for sixteen years and integrated psychodramatic techniques into other classes such as Techniques of Counseling, Group Counseling, Theories of Counseling, and Practicum. He used psychodrama methods with clients in his private practice with individuals and families. His experience with psychodrama à deux motivated him to write this book.

Dr. Knittel received recognition at state and national levels for his efforts to improve standards of excellence in the counseling and teaching professions. He also received leadership and teaching awards throughout his career, including the Pratt-Heinz award for excellence in teaching in 1987, given by the university to the outstanding teacher of the year.

He contributed chapters for two of Dr. Paul Welter's books as well as various articles for state and national counseling periodicals. He conducted workshops during his thirty-plus years at the university in the areas of psychodrama, parent-child relationships, individual and group counseling, and teaching methods. He published Strategies for Directing Psychodrama with the Adolescent in the *Journal of Group Psychotherapy, Psychodrama, & Sociometry* (Fall 1990) and presented numerous papers on psychodrama at state and national conferences. He published "Hanging On and Letting Go: The Parent's Dilemma" in *Counseling*

Today (March 2007) and Empty Chair Grief Work from a Psychodramatic Perspective (Spring 2010), an American Counseling Association publication. He also published Counseling Optimists and Pessimists in *Counseling Today* (October 2009). He published Lessons of a Lifetime in *inMotion*, a publication of the Amputee Coalition of America. He published his autobiography Life Is Not Random in 2006.

FOREWORD

The following is from Dr. John Nolte, a psychodrama practitioner and trainer for over forty years. He was my mentor during my psychodrama training. His Ph. D. is in clinical psychology from Washington University, and he was trained in psychodrama by J. L. Moreno and Zerka Moreno. He is a certified trainer/educator/ practitioner by the American Board of Examiners in Psychodrama, Sociometry, and Group Psychotherapy. He is a recognized expert and senior practitioner in psychodrama. He has published numerous articles, and his most recent book is The Psychodrama Papers (2008). He has presented papers and workshops throughout the world.

Dr. Nolte has held appointments in the departments of mental health in Missouri and Illinois. He is a charter member of the faculty of Sangamon State University, which offered psychodrama in a number of Midwest cities. He established the National Psychodrama Training Center that serves clients coast to coast.

To whom it may concern,

Psychodrama is a wonderful and effective method as everybody who has experienced it either as subject (protagonist) or practitioner (director) will attest. Known primarily in the field of mental health and counseling, even usually defined as "a method of psychotherapy," psychodrama has many nonclinical applications as well. And it is woefully underutilized in both its clinical and nonclinical uses. In *Counseling and Drama: Psychodrama 'A Duex*, Dr. Marvin Knittel has produced a valuable addition to the psychodrama literature for counselors who have never tried action methods. I strongly hope that his work will persuade a lot of counselors to become acquainted with, utilize, and get training in psychodrama.

The first rule of psychodrama is "Don't tell me; *show* me." Dr. Knittel follows that rule in his presentation of the psychodrama method in this book. He *shows* us how he applies the method in his counseling room, taking us through nine sessions step-by-step. We can practically visualize the process. And the case studies he presents are varied and often quite moving.

The reader may notice that there is very little clinical vocabulary in the case studies, other than an occasional mention of a diagnosis by a referring mental health professional. This is because the psychodrama method, explained by Dr. Knittel, is a normative method (like the other great counseling approach devised by Carl Rogers) and holds that problems are not usually the result of pathology but occur when something is getting in the way of somebody's natural ability to solve them. I think that Dr. Knittel's case studies not only make that clear, but also are testimonials to that holistic position.

In the interests of disclosure, I need to note that Marvin Knittel attended many psychodrama workshops, which I conducted in Omaha, Nebraska. He mentions that in the book. A teacher's greatest joy is seeing a student make a significant achievement. With this book, Marv makes me proud to have been one of his trainers.

Sincerely,
John Nolte, Ph. D., T.E.P.

The following is from Marlene Kuskie, Ed. D., who is a professor of counseling and school psychology on the graduate faculty of the University of Nebraska-Kearney. She is a nationally certified counselor, licensed professional counselor, and mental health counselor in the state of Nebraska. She has published ten referred journal articles and presented thirty-six papers at national and state conferences. She consults widely and specializes in family counseling.

To whom it may concern,

Counselors are always seeking new and more effective interventions to invite change and provide encouragement for their clients. Psychodrama enriches the process and encourages the process of change. Dr. Knittel has taken the counseling intervention of psychodrama to a new level by making it practical, interesting, and possible for the beginning and experienced counselor to use. The reader will become aware of the principles and the psychodrama process through specific examples of clients. Dr. Knittel shares his wealth of knowledge and experience concerning counseling issues and psychodrama within the stories. The reader will be encouraged to use the ideas and techniques and will discover the energy of change that comes from psychodrama. Dr. Knittel's description encourages the counselor and the client to be creative and to experience new meanings from old situations.

The following is from Mr. James Nelson who has published nine books. His most recent is on the history of Tombstone, Arizona. He has served as editor of books for several other writers.

To whom it may concern,

It takes a great deal of courage to submit a manuscript to another author for comment. When Marv Knittel asked me to review his first work, an autobiography, I agreed with a degree of trepidation. Marv is a good friend, and I truly dreaded being put in the position of equivocating. I was pleased to find an enthralling story of his life, well constructed and fun to read.

Consequently, when he asked me to take a look at Counseling and Drama Psychodrama 'A Deux, I readily agreed. As I anticipated, the manuscript was very readable. However, it was the subject matter that truly captivated me. I knew nothing at all about psychodrama, and I was truly fascinated by the techniques used and especially the results of the process. I am delighted to recommend this book. It is one of those rare educational works that is a pleasure to read.

James Nelson

PREFACE

This book deals with action methods of counseling when working one-on-one or with a family. Psychodrama, its origin, and how it fits within the field of counseling is explained. There is a review of selected publications that describe the use of psychodrama in individual counseling—psychodrama à deux. The core of the book is the nine case studies that demonstrate how psychodrama is used à deux.

A limited number of publications exclusively devoted to explaining how psychodrama is used with one-on-one counseling were found and are summarized. They reflect divergent opinions that prompted me to write this book for the seasoned professional counselor in the field and for students in training.

This book is unique because it shows how psychodrama is used one-on-one with clients while maintaining the boundary between the counselor and the client. The counselor does not inject himself into the drama as an auxiliary or a double, which is frequently done by many who attempt to do psychodrama à deux.

ACKNOWLEDGMENTS

A host of people have influenced my writing on this subject. I am grateful to every graduate student who took my psychodrama classes when I was a professor in the Department of Counseling and School Psychology at the University of Nebraska-Kearney. It was there that I demonstrated and tested almost every psychodrama method. The student's validation of this powerful method encouraged me to organize my thoughts concerning psychodrama with one-on-one counseling.

Dr. John Nolte influenced my love of psychodrama. He periodically came to the Midwest Psychodrama Training Center in Omaha, Nebraska, and patiently led the groups through applications of psychodrama methods and explained the basic philosophy of J. L. Moreno. Since then, the training center has been renamed the National Psychodrama Training Center and presents training in a large geographical area. Dr. Nolte is one of a handful of scholars who truly understands the works of Moreno. I am indebted to John for his help editing the book. I value his encouragement.

I thank my wife, Dearwyn, for instinctively knowing when to be patient while I wrote. She is the one who edited and reedited the numerous drafts. I also appreciate the advice and encouragement from my friend and writer Jim Nelson.

CHAPTER ONE

PSYCHODRAMA

Two friends sit at the kitchen table surrounded by silence. One quietly gazes down at the table, holding a cup of coffee as if warming the chill from her hands. Her friend sees the quiet desperation and says, "You have something heavy on your mind this morning. Do you need to talk?" Friends have been helping each other since the beginning of man's existence, and we are driven to understand how our mind functions and create methods to treat each other. From Joseph Gall's *phrenology* in the early 1800s to the present time, our quest has been to create methods of counseling or psychotherapy that will relieve the burdened and bewildered.

There are almost as many definitions of counseling as there are counselors. The term counseling was originally used by Frank Parsons in 1908 and was adopted by Carl Rogers. Various identities are attached to the strategies for helping clients. There are clinical psychologists, counseling psychologists, marriage counselors, school counselors, vocational counselors, rehabilitation counselors, genetic counselors, and many more. Counseling can be for personal, social, vocational, educational, and empowerment concerns (Gladding 1996).

To complicate things even more, *coaching* has emerged from management consulting and leadership training. One way to understand the progression from psychotherapy to counseling to coaching is to move along a continuum beginning with pathologically oriented psychoanalysis, to psychotherapy concerned with unconscious motives, to counseling concerned with issues of adjustment in a client's present life. Coaching tends to be future-oriented and goal-focused. Methods presented in this book relate to psychodrama.

Most counseling is two-dimensional. That is, a client describes his or her life, while a counselor listens. Metaphorically, a client throws his or her emotional paint onto a canvass, reflecting the random and confused nature of his or her feelings or thoughts. The counselor looks for a pattern that can shed light on the client's unhappiness, grief, sorrow, misery, desolation, or despondency. Together they discover patterns, search for solutions, and create a plan for growth. Nevertheless, the "canvass" remains two-dimensional.

Psychodrama is a method of group and individual counseling that bypasses the traditional talk therapy. Moreno suggested that time and space are neglected dimensions in most therapies. He wrote, "Thus all three dimensions of time—past, present and future are brought together in psychodrama." He continues, "The idea of psychotherapy of space has been pioneered by psychodrama, which is action-centered and comprehensively tries to integrate all the dimensions of living into itself" (Moreno 1969, 3:13). The client enters a three-dimensional sphere of counseling that can bring the past and future into the present. Therefore, counseling in the third dimensions of time and space permit clients to examine life by creating a new paradigm by examining scenes and settings that bring the past or future into the present. This surplus reality helps the client to not only see the "canvass," but also step into the painting and experience or reexperience life in all of its dimensions.

More than fifty years ago, Dr. Wilder Penfield, a Canadian neurologist, gave mild electrode stimulation to a patient's brain. The patient subsequently recalled past events in detail. Of significance was Penfield's discovery that the event was stored *along with the feelings* associated with the event. They are locked together so that one cannot be evoked without the other. The brain records and plays back in high fidelity. Dr. Penfield found that experiences can be recalled and also relived.

It is logical, therefore, that feelings are recorded with the experience—accurate or inaccurate. Psychodrama, thus, becomes a significant method to unlock feelings from the experience in order to reexamine, validate, and reframe emotions.

For example, assume a father convinces his four-year-old daughter that she is responsible for her mother's death in spite of evidence to the contrary. The accusation of the father is a voice-over with which the daughter lives. Now suppose the daughter is twenty-four years old and begins to question her guilt. Rather than only talking about her experiences, she can psychodramatically step into time and space to candidly confront her absent father through a dyadic psychodramatic encounter. She can create an accurate voice-over reflecting her innocence. She can spontaneously add a new soundtrack with new information to the video of her life. She can delete or modify the old inaccurate script by replacing it with a new more accurate script. Although she cannot change the past, she *can* change her life script.

CHAPTER TWO

PSYCHODRAMA AND OTHER METHODS

This chapter clarifies the history and basic theory of psychodrama and compares other theorists with Moreno. Moreno developed a method of therapy that addresses client issues in the moment rather than searching for repressed pathology. Zerka Moreno reported in an interview with Victor Yalom, "He [J. L. Moreno] was anti-analytic. He did not believe in Freud's model. Freud came from biology. Moreno was inspired by the great religions of this world" (Yalom 2000).

In 1912, Moreno attended one of Freud's lectures on analysis. Moreno reported, "As the students filed out, he [Freud] singled me out from the crowd and asked me what I was doing. I responded 'Well Dr. Freud, I start where you leave off. You meet people in the artificial setting of your office. I meet them on the street and in their homes, in their natural surroundings. You analyze their dreams. I give them the courage to dream again. You analyze and tear them apart. I let them act out their conflicting roles and help them to put the parts together again'" (Moreno 1989). At the time of the encounter, Moreno was twenty years old while Freud was fifty-six. I can only imagine what Freud thought when he heard the words "act out" because it meant something quite different for the two men. The encounter also gives a partial view into the confidence, conviction, and perhaps audacity of Moreno.

Moreno had a cosmological view of mankind. He held visions for mankind and society that propelled him to be a conduit for change. His sense of responsibility to create a spontaneous-creative order frustrated him most of his life. He was a man ahead of his time. Nevertheless, he was the driving influence for the creation of psychodrama at Beacon, St. Elizabeth's Hospital, and the Harvard Psychodrama Theatre to name only three (Marineau 1989).

I was fortunate to learn about psychodrama from Dr. John Nolte, a student of J. L. Moreno. Nolte writes, "There is no scientific definition of genius, but there is no question in my mind that Moreno fits the description" (Nolte 2008, 271). A genius sees and internalizes things differently than most other people do. Nolte goes on to write, "With a few exceptions, most applications of Morenean methods and theory are in one field, mental health, and almost nobody identifies actively with Moreno's original goal of bringing about a spontaneous creative social order" (Nolte 2008, 278).

Spontaneity and Creativity

"Moreno's notion of spontaneity-creativity is the foundation stone of all of his major theories and methods" (Nolte 2008, 109). Moreno writes in a 1955 issue of *Sociometry*, "I formulated this twin concept as the primary principles of existence in my earliest efforts [*Das Testament des Vaters*] to comprehend the living universe in its entirety" (From Nolte, p. 106).

The concept of spontaneity-creativity has been further described by Moreno in *Who Shall Survive* and referenced in *Psychodrama* volume 2 (1975). He wrote, "Spontaneity is difficult to define but this does not relieve us from asking what its meaning is. An important source of information are [*sic*] the experiences from one's personal, subjective life" (Moreno, 1:137). Moreno wrote that he discovered the spontaneous man for the first time at the age of four when he and his friends piled chairs to the basement ceiling and Moreno fell from the top chair, breaking his arm. He tells he discovered the spontaneous man again at age seventeen when he could not deliver his prepared speech. "I realized that it would be unfair to the moment and to the people surrounding me not to share the moment with them and not express myself as the situation and the present needs of the people required." He adds that he discovered the spontaneous man again during the thousands of psychodrama sessions because he was drawn into working in the *here and now*. He ends his brief discussion saying, "The last time I discovered the spontaneous man again was when I began to work with our son Jonathan's role reversals" (Moreno, 1:137). Notions of staying in the here and now are held by several other models of counseling including the existential models, Glasser's Reality Therapy, and cognitive-behavioral therapies (Corey 1996).

Spontaneity is occurring within the moment we meet a new situation adequately and appropriately or an old situation with new energy and strength. Spontaneity-creativity is experienced intuitively and instinctively in the moment of existence. The phenomenon is illusive. That is, we are "in the moment," enveloped by a discovery that moves us into a realm not unlike an altered state of consciousness. We have spontaneously created a new window through which to view the universe and our existence. The experience in the moment surrounds us as a bubble surrounds the space within. Most of us, for example, have glimpsed that moment when we are shown a drawing that morphs into another drawing while we gaze at it. You may recall drawings that we initially see from the top down, but after a moment, we see it from the bottom up. We have an "aha" experience. Although that is not a spontaneous-creative experience, it is something that transcends logic and seems beyond our control and provides a peek into spontaneity. Synthesizing old knowledge into something new is creative. Perhaps we form a new gestalt in which the whole is more than the sum of the parts. Perls (Gestalt therapy) created conditions that led clients to find new ways to confront old situations. Then again, Perls may have found his inspiration from Moreno. Dr. Stephan Tobin, a clinical psychologist who uses Gestalt therapy in his practice, studied under Perls. Dr. Tobin related in an e-mail to me that Fritz Perls had contact with Moreno and "got some of his ideas from him" (Tobin 2008). Tobin also related that Perls was very interested in the theater as a young man. Perls once told Tobin that when he was at Esalen, he saw himself as more of a director than a therapist.

When we direct a psychodrama and join the protagonist on his or her journey of discovery, we witness the phenomenon of spontaneity-creativity. As a director/therapist, we experience tele as we join the world of another. Something new emerges that forever changes the past, present, and future. The protagonist discovers the change by looking back from the present. Thus, creativity catalyzed by spontaneity is understood most clearly in retrospect.

Cultural Conserve

The end product of a creative act is a *conserve*. "Anything that has been created, everything that can be named or identified is a conserve" (Nolte, p. 123). Subsets resulting from human creativity are called *cultural conserves* and provide the foundation for culture and society, according to Moreno. Conserves, such as the printed page, the musical composition, mathematical formulas, letters, words, etc., all hold us in place, providing predictable and recurring conditions in life. Without the anchor of a conserve, life is filled with anxiety.

However, if we are dominated by conserves, there is no change. "Through psychodrama, protagonists not only can free themselves from conserves but can also explore their process of warming up to problematic emotions, relationships, conserves or situations which interfere with creative living" (Nolte, p. 131). A protagonist can confront old issues in a new way through the action of psychodrama. The reality, however, is that a new conserve evolves from the creative act! Moreno writes, "Spontaneity functions only in the moment of its emergence just as, metaphorically speaking, light is turned on in a room, and all parts of it are distinct. When the light was turned off in a room, the basic structure remained the same, but a fundamental quality disappeared" (Moreno 1977, vol. 1).

Cultural conserves are also challenged through the method of reality therapy. Glasser, the founder of reality therapy, describes that we each approach life with a set of perceptions with which we try to ascribe meaning to our existence. He metaphorically describes that in our heads, we each create a personal album of pictures representing the world we wish for. As we encounter conditions that do not fit the picture, we may experience anxiety and agitation. At that point we either reorganize our "album" or try, often in vain, to change our experience to fit the picture. Moreno's conserve is similar to Glasser's notion of an album. Reality therapy may not refer to surplus reality or use action-oriented methods, but clients confront reality and assume responsibility for change. When the picture changes, the person experiences a new balance or as Moreno might say, "equilibrium," and a new role emerges because the conserve has been modified.

Catharsis

Cathartic therapy evolved during the early 1900s when Breuer and Freud observed release of suppressed personal material under hypnosis from a woman referred to as Anna O. Later, Freud rejected catharsis as a therapeutic tool and developed insight-driven psychoanalysis (Brill 1995). Freud introduced the term *abreaction*, which Freud described as an expression of a repressed traumatic experience. He later deemphasized abreaction as well as catharsis because he felt they were of temporary help. Nevertheless, clients experience catharsis when suppressed feelings find their way to the light in the moment of therapy. Few people distinguish catharsis from abreaction (Nolte 2008).

Catharsis is another important element of Moreno's psychodramatic theory. *Webster's Dictionary* defines catharsis as a technique used in psychology to relieve tension and anxiety by bringing repressed feelings and fears to consciousness. The term comes from the ancient Greeks—specifically from Aristotle. Greek drama enabled members of the audience to experience a catharsis when they identified with some action in the play. Catharsis becomes the dramatic clarification and explanation. The therapeutic result of this process is abreaction. That is, the purging of self-defeating assumptions that have interfered with personal integration. In other words, according to the psychoanalytic theory, a cathartic release weakens or eliminates the anxiety of the original anxiety-provoking experience. The repressed material is purged from the unconscious to the conscious level, producing the healing effect.

This catharsis of integration returns the client to a state of equilibrium, moving the client away from disequilibrium that hinders a satisfactory response to life situations. The catharsis, therefore, can change the conserve that framed the client's interpretation of life events. Thus, catharsis opens a client to more likely experience spontaneity-creativity.

Fritz Perls, through Gestalt therapy, provided opportunities for clients to experience catharsis and return to a state of equilibrium by experiencing the moment. He believed meaning comes from experiencing the moment unencumbered by the past. Perls placed the client into experiential situations such as self-dialogue, enactment and dramatization, guided fantasy, monodrama, and empty-chair technique. These seem to be psychodramatic in origin but differ in that psychodrama follows the lead of the client (protagonist), while Perls and others who use psychodramatic principles follow the lead of the therapist. Nevertheless, Gestalt and existentialistic therapies use the cathartic technique to help clients release controlled emotions.

Surplus Reality

Moreno wrote what I believe to be the clearest explanation of the psychodramatic experience. He wrote, "A therapeutic situation is needed in which reality can be simulated, so that people can learn to develop new techniques of living without risking serious consequences or disaster, as they might in life itself" (Moreno 1975, 1:15).

The idea of "not risking serious consequences" is extraordinarily important and sets psychodrama apart from the majority of therapies that encourage clients to confront serious concerns in real time. For example, I know counselors who encourage a client to find the sexual perpetrator and confront him directly. The risk is very high because the result may exacerbate the problem when the narcissistic perpetrator denies and shifts the responsibility back to the victim.

Thus Moreno created an intangible, invisible dimension of intra—and extra-psychic life called "surplus reality" for the psychodramatic journey. Surplus reality in the moment is as real as the morning sunrise but protected from dangerous ultraviolet rays. It is safe and can be stopped and started to examine the reality of the moment. No other therapeutic method offers such potential to free us from a cultural conserve that may inhibit spontaneity from being the catalyst for creativity.

Zerka Moreno declared in her interview with Yalom that "psychodrama is improvisational drama. Which is the way we live in life" (Yalom 2000). She tells of a patient who says, "I know what psychodrama is: it's the double of life" (Moreno et al. 2000). Moreno continued, "The double life! In other words, you can have one life and another life in psychodrama." Other action-oriented counseling and therapeutic approaches take advantage of the power of the moment but do not possess the structure of psychodrama. Some of these are art therapy, dance therapy, drama therapy, play therapy, primal therapy, Eye Movement Desensitization and Reprocessing (EMDR), expressive therapy, Gestalt therapy, holding therapy, T-groups, and others. These are usually therapist-controlled approaches. They generally do not utilize role reversal.

Role Reversal

Moreno states, "One of the most popular surplus reality techniques in psychodrama is that of *role reversal*" (Moreno 1975, 3:16). Role reversal provides a safe way to examine all the roles we play with significant people in our lives and discover how a new role might feel. Through the process of role reversal, the protagonist can benefit from an encounter without the risk of a live meeting. We all assume different roles during our lifetime by modeling or experimenting. Integration of these roles reflects who we become.

This self-examination occurs in other counseling methods albeit without the structure of psychodrama. For example, Gestalt therapy uses several techniques to accomplish the task of role examination with monodrama, guided fantasy, self-dialogue, and the empty-chair technique. Psychodrama and Gestalt therapy work in the present and bring the client to an awareness of self (Latner 1992). Perls was an observer of psychodrama and adopted the "hot seat" idea from Moreno. Another Gestalt approach is called the "empty chair." The significant difference between the Gestalt technique is that the therapist will designate an empty chair and suggest to the client, "Imagine [name someone] is there in the chair. Now, say what you wish to him/her." In psychodrama, *imagine* dilutes the power. Role reversal with the person in the empty chair creates the presence of the absent person, creating surplus reality in a three-dimensional context. It matters not if the chair is empty or occupied by an auxiliary.

Psychodramatic Roles

Tian Dayton reminds us that the basic roles of psychodrama are the *protagonist* whose story is enacted; the *double* or the inner voice of the protagonist; the *director* who is the therapist who manages the drama; the *auxiliary egos* who are people in the group who play needed characters in the drama; and the *audience* who are the group witnessing the drama and benefiting from the story (Dayton 1994, 8). There are experiential and action-oriented therapies offered to the public; most of which follow the lead of the therapist whereas psychodrama follows the lead of the client. The protagonist controls but the director orchestrates.

Transactional Analysis, conceived by Eric Berne, presents the formulation of three ego states: Parent, Adult, and Child with the *parent ego state* representing rules to live by; the *adult ego state* representing the analyzer; and the *child ego state* representing the playful natural child, the creative little professor or the guilty and shameful adaptive child. These easily understood concepts became popular ways to understand the roles people play in relationships. The psychologically unsophisticated consumer is able to identify his or her ego state and begins to understand his or her own behavior. The ego states are roles that help people understand relationships. The role of parent, adult, or child can become a conserve (in Morenean terms) and may create disequilibrium affecting others. Harris picked up the banner with his book, *I'm OK—You're OK* (Harris 1969). Harris successfully wrote a practical guide to transactional analysis. Transactions enlighten all of us about reasons relations are functional or dysfunctional. Berne acknowledged Moreno for methods that shaped part of transactional analysis.

Even behavioral counseling such as Albert Ellis's *rational emotive behavior therapy* could not ignore the roles people play. He concerned himself with teaching clients to change the way they think and behave by modifying their self-descriptions. He was conscious that the roles we take can be self-destructing or self-edifying. However, it is unlikely that Ellis would have embraced the action phase of psychodrama. Particularly difficult would be the concepts of spontaneity-creativity and abreaction. Ellis seemed to want much more control of the thinking and behavior than psychodrama endorses.

On the other hand, narrative therapy may be more compatible with the objectives of psychodrama than most other counseling methods. It was initially developed in the 1970s and 1980s by Michael White and David Epston. It became widely known in North America with the publication of their book *Narrative Means to Therapeutic Ends* in 1990 (Epston and White 1990). The goal of narrative therapy is to objectify, that is externalize, problems with stories or narratives from the client. The problem moves from inside to outside, making it easier for the client to investigate. Events are examined, and the client realizes the "problem" is much larger than the "self." He or she is encouraged to "rewrite" or "restory" the experience. By being the "investigative reporter," the client explores alternative outcomes to the dilemma. The counselor functions more as a guide than an influential tactician. The client remains focused in the here and now rather than searching for the pathology of history. Finally, the counselor may use other people as "outside witnesses" from whom the client learns to view the problem through a different window.

An examination of narrative therapy shows that it is similar to psychodrama in that the counselor assumes the role of facilitator apposed to regulator. The client is free to discover the nature of the disequilibrium without being told or led into an area to which the client has not yet been warmed up. It has neither the action phase nor the degree of structure evident in psychodrama, but interaction with one or more people helping "restory" the problem uses the group that is suggestive of psychodrama. The downside of narrative therapy is that the counselor is in a position of exerting considerable influence and that there is a lack of research to substantiate the claims of efficacy.

Carl Rogers would embrace the conditions created through psychodrama that allows personal growth and self-actualization. He believed that the relationship between the client and counselor cleared the way for growth. Rogers's concept of a counseling relationship is not unlike *tele* described by Moreno. That is, seeing eye to eye in a relationship that creates the moment as the singular overwhelming experience. In a similar way, the director orchestrates a drama that clears away the clutter that allows for something new to evolve. Both Rogers and Moreno focused on nonpathology and believed change occurs in the here and now. The present moment was paramount to both of them.

Solution-focused therapy of de Shazer and Berg is linked to a host of behavior therapies and so-called brief therapies. The focus is to increase behaviors that work and eliminate behaviors that do not work. The emphasis on normative behavior and staying in the moment resonates with psychodrama. The structure of psychodrama is far more complex than most solution-focused counseling are, but both counseling approaches are focused on the solution rather than the problem.

Viktor Frankl survived the concentration camps of WW II and was moved by his experience to develop logotherapy. Logotherapists listen for meaninglessness in the life of a client. They look for healthy attitudes and work toward reduction in symptoms. Logotherapists believe meaning is discovered, not given. Again, psychodrama and logotherapy focus on the here and now and discovery and are not driven by pathology. The logotherapist challenges with questions while psychodrama reveals the question in role reversal in surplus reality.

In summary, psychodrama is an ingenious method soundly anchored in the theoretical foundation of spontaneity-creativity, surplus reality, and creating equilibrium out of disequilibrium. Other counseling methods focus on role definition and change, but few incorporate the elements of action found in psychodrama.

The next chapter explains the use of psychodrama with individuals one-on-one. Psychodramatic techniques will be modified to account for the absence of a third person in the session. Attention is given to warm-up, action, and sharing. These three parts of a drama assure the readiness of the protagonist, the journey of the protagonist, and sharing which helps the protagonist integrate the action and seek closure. Psychodrama à deux is not a method intended for every issue, but it is a method that fits a large number of client concerns.

CHAPTER THREE

PSYCHODRAMA À DEUX

Moreno recognized psychodrama à deux as a valid therapeutic method. He wrote, "It should be remembered that psychodrama and group psychotherapy are two independent developments. Contrary to unsophisticated opinion, psychodrama is the broader classification. Individual, "a deux," psychodrama is possible; it is an accepted and valuable form of psychotherapy, but obviously "individual" group psychotherapy is a contradiction" (Moreno 1973, 24).

The core of this book is about applying psychodramatic methods to counseling one client at a time in a counselor's office and a family in their home or in the counselor's office. My psychodrama training was with a group. Other trainees were available as an audience and to serve as auxiliaries for role reversals, doubling, mirroring, and other roles in the psychodrama. During my years in private practice, I occasionally conducted weekend psychodrama retreats for groups, but my private practice was primarily with individuals.

When I work one-on-one with clients, I use a variety of methods that include client-centered counseling, Gestalt therapy, rational emotive behavior therapy, reality therapy, solution-focused counseling, guided imagery, as well as psychodrama à deux. I find that psychodrama à deux used with guided imagery is a very effective method of counseling for a wide range of client issues. Of course, a host of auxiliaries would be helpful; however, that is impossible when I am helping a client alone in my office. I discover clients have an amazing capacity for creativity. I find psychodrama is only limited by the creativity and spontaneity of the client and the counselor.

The case studies reported in the remaining chapters show how to utilize the following techniques à deux: *director, protagonist, auxiliary ego, empty chair, scene setting, role reversal, double, multiple double, mirroring, soliloquy, tele, concretization,*

---

catharsis of abreaction, catharsis of integration, warm-up, action, and *sharing.* My philosophy of directing one-on-one psychodrama is the result of research and years of using psychodrama à deux in my office. The conclusions are relatively simple:

- Spontaneity-creativity and surplus reality are keys to a successful psychodrama à deux.
- Role reversal, role playing, and role taking are central to the process.
- The director is accepting, genuine, congruent, and empathetic.
- The director does not patronize the protagonist and respects his or her autonomy.
- The director must mentally explore hypothetical directions of the drama while trusting the drama as the final arbiter.
- The client has the capacity to assimilate new data and find his or her own equilibrium.
- The client presents truth as he or she perceives it.
- Action is in the here and now regardless of when the actual incident took place.
- The client selects the time and place for the action phase of the drama.
- The director must appropriately pace the drama to reflect client needs.
- The client should act out rather than talk about his or her conflicts.
- The client is responsible for his or her choices.

Most important, the director stays in the role of director throughout the session and resists assuming auxiliary roles. The director remains the anchor and manager and orchestrates the drama. Moreno wrote, "The psychodramatic director has three functions: (a) he is a producer, (b) chief therapist, and (3) social analyst" (Moreno 1972, 1:252).

John Casson (1997) reported in his publication *Psychodrama in Individual Psychotherapy* that "there are very few references to psychodrama a deux in the literature that are available." He went on, "The most extensive writing on psychodrama a deux is in David Kipper's book *Psychotherapy Through Role Playing*" (1986). I found twelve out of 365 pages by Kipper devoted to psychodrama à deux. Kipper writes, "If clinical role playing is to be used in individual therapy, the therapist will have to participate as an auxiliary and assume various roles in the life of the protagonist" (Kipper, p. 340). He defends psychodrama (dramatherapy) for individuals when the individual is disinclined to be in a group and when an individual is concerned with privacy. The director assuming the role of an auxiliary runs counter to my experience and philosophy.

I found disagreement among the authors and disagreement with my philosophy and methods of psychodrama à deux. Marcia Stein and Monica Callahan support Casson's observation that little is written about psychodrama à deux. They wrote that "psychodramatists themselves have occasionally worked with individuals although this is seldom mentioned in the literature" (1974, 120). Stein and Callahan go on to write, "Few studies, however, specifically emphasize the use of action methods in the treatment of individuals" (1974, 120). They advocate that the director play the roles of both auxiliary ego and director. However, they concede that "the client can double herself" (p.122). They suggest that during *mirroring*, the director reenact the scene. You will read in a case study I report later in this book that mirroring can be done by using guided imagery. They support role reversal as an acceptable and appropriate technique for psychodrama à deux, as do the other writers including Kipper, Casson, Vander May, Landy, and Cukier.

Robert Landy wrote chapter 7 in Jennings' book, *Dramatherapy: Theory and Practice* (Jennings 1992). Landy's chapter is titled "The Role of the Dramatherapist Working with Individuals One-on-One" (1992). My experience with dramatherapy is meager, which may account for my difficulty reading Landy's chapter. He states, "A dramatherapy group experience can be quite dizzying as projected roles dart about, bat-like." He goes on to say, "The role of the dramatherapist changes in a one-on-one situation, or rather, it expands" (1992, 99). He goes on to discuss distancing and underdistancing. He frequently addresses boundaries and separation between counselor and client. He concludes with, "Working one-on-one is fairly new to me" (1992, 107). Suggestions of how to work one-on-one with clients is limited.

There are numerous ways to utilize the majority of psychodramatic techniques with individuals. I was pleased to read the paper by James Vander May published on the Adam Blatner Web site on May 21, 2008. He offered a description of several techniques such as role reversal, future projection, scene setting, soliloquy, auxiliary chair. However, he advocated the need for a third person to concretize a feeling. There are other ways to concretize abstract feelings for a client, however. I also think there are ways to double and mirror without the director moving out of role. He admits, "It becomes easy to lose track of who is in what role." That is precisely why I make it a rule in psychodrama à deux to keep the director in the role of director even if some psychodramatic techniques are compromised. Overall, however, I found Vander May's paper to be valuable.

Dr. Dale Buchanan and Dr. Antonina Garcia presented an essay titled "Psychodrama in Individual Therapy: Psychodrama À Deux" on their Psychodrama Training Associates Internet page. Buchanan and Garcia refer the reader to Stein and Callahan's publication in the 1982 fall issue of Journal of Group Psychotherapy Psychodrama & Sociometry (JGPPS) as an excellent resource for one-on-one therapy. My review of Stein and Callahan suggests they advocate that the director frequently play the role of an absent person and function as double.

Buchanan and Garcia devote a healthy portion of their article to helping a client warm up to action. Their suggestions are useful. They remind us of the need to keep the drama in the here and now, which also appeared in the other publications. The publications I reviewed on psychodrama à deux had a common view about scene setting. They all agreed a client must have a sense of being present in the moment—whether the moment is past, present, or future.

Buchanan and Garcia are the only writers in my review who introduced the concept of using wisdom figures to enhance the drama. I also was impressed that they conceived of the multiple doubles without necessarily utilizing the director to assume a position in any chair during the doubling process. They did suggest the director could enhance the intensity by expressing a more compelling phrase from one of the "inner" doubles.

The element of "atonement" useful in psychodrama is not unique with individual psychodrama. They suggested some very insightful techniques for psychodrama à deux. Among them were the high chair, metaphors, myths, magic shop, and dream reenactment, to name a few.

I think Buchanan and Garcia believe the director should refrain from becoming an auxiliary. I recommend their work because they make a clear distinction between group psychodrama and psychodrama à deux.

Rosa Cukier (2007) wrote *Bipersonal Psychodrama: Its Techniques, Therapists, and Clients*. Cukier is a Brazilian psychologist and psychotherapist with specializations in psychoanalysis and psychodrama. Her introduction to the book is, "[It is] intended to describe a number of therapeutic procedures which could be used in bipersonal psychodrama" (Cukier 2007, 2). She chooses the term *bipersonal psychodrama* to represent psychodrama therapies that do not employ auxiliary egos. She writes, "Moreno's psychodrama consisted mainly in therapeutic acts and not in therapeutic processes, like the ones we perform nowadays." This assertion is not in agreement with that of Casson, Landy, Buchanan and Garcia, Stein and Callahan, Vander May, or Kipper.

Cukier writes that bipersonal psychodrama "represents a throwback. Starting with Moreno, we see that he seldom mentions this technical possibility, and when he does, it is in a somewhat derogatory manner." Following that statement, she writes that J. L. and Zerka Moreno suggest psychodrama à deux is parallel to psychoanalysis on the couch and that the therapist "in private practice frequently prefers to employ his nurse as an auxiliary ego to maintain his own identity as director unimpaired" (Moreno, 2:232). The quotation is correct but must be taken within the context of other Moreno writings.

Cukier's book lacks the specificity for bipersonal psychodrama that I had hoped for. She advocates that the therapist be actively involved in role play with the client. She prefers to use the interview technique. She writes, "I prefer to use the interview technique, which allows me the mobility of coming and going between the client's fantasy and the session's reality" (p.19). Dialogue is the primary way Cukier helps the client assimilate the psychodramatic techniques.

She approaches the empty-chair technique the way a Gestaltist does by asking him to *imagine* that a person sitting on the chair is the one with whom he has something to talk about, or parts of him he would like to work on.

I found Cukier's book to be a rather superficial treatment of psychodrama à deux. The adaptations simply give the therapist a dual role. The result creates "three" people for therapy and essentially ignores the concept of à deux.

John Casson in his 1997 article on psychodrama in individual psychotherapy reports on the "recently discovered Howell tape" that Moreno said, "Psychodrama can be done also on an individual basis. You can do psychodrama a deux." Moreno went on to say, "You are on a stage in action, in a series of actions. Psychodrama is really more inclusive than group psychotherapy" (Casson 1997; from the Howell tape).

In summary, it was either explicit or implicit from all of the writers that the success of psychodrama à deux rests on a sound, genuine, congruent, and respectful relationship with the client. The extent to which the therapist becomes directly involved by assuming an auxiliary role ranged from Buchanan and Garcia (the least) to Cukier (the most). Most of them correctly understood the position taken by Moreno. All of them placed role reversal at the center of the action, but they were not in agreement regarding the degree of participation of the therapist. They seemed to understand that spontaneity-creativity along with surplus reality lies at the center of Moreno's theory. They were not equally articulate concerning what these concepts are about. There was some confusion about concretization. Some believed the technique requires an auxiliary, and some saw beyond the boundary and considered other alternatives. I was gratified that they believed mirroring, doubling, and multiple doubling can be done à deux.

Rebecca Walters of the Hudson Valley Psychodrama Institute in New Paltz, New York, wrote her master's thesis on psychodrama à deux and wrote in an e-mail to me about the lack of books on psychodrama à deux, "There isn't anything else out there except for articles here and there" (October 2009).

Introduction to Case Studies

The following chapters are samples of case studies from my practice that apply psychodrama in a one-on-one counseling setting. The chapters cover the following: *search for meaning, sexual abuse, unfinished business, depression, hanging on and letting go, dependency, family issues, aging,* and *unresolved guilt.* I will introduce the case and prep the reader about the methods employed with the client or clients. Details of the dialogue between the client and the therapist are presented along with rationale for therapeutic interventions. I will walk the reader through each of these cases and describe in detail how to use psychodrama without the presence of a group. I have italicized each specific technique I wish to emphasize.

Chapter Four

SEARCH FOR MEANING

This chapter introduces the reader to *role reversal* in a surreal setting. The client experiences the unlikely situation of conversing with himself after his own death. The client discovers his own wisdom without the distractions of real time or space.

George is forty-five years old and has been in group therapy. He is troubled that even in his midyears he continues to struggle with meaning in his life. As we begin to talk, George explains his empty feelings of existence and that he wants his life to have meaning. Unsure of how to describe his feelings, he says, "All I know is I feel empty." It is possible to key on the word *empty* and allow the client to dramatize what empty is for him. I have chosen to key on his broader meaning of futility or lack of meaning.

I say to George, "Since we usually see things clearly in hindsight, perhaps you may discover your illusive answers by looking back from the end of your life." I continue, "We can begin your search by attending your own funeral." He gives me one of those looks reserved for people one suit short of a full deck.

We create the funeral scene where the *action* takes place. George sees himself in a three-dimensional mortuary where he captures the sensation of time and space. To help George *set the scene*, I say, "We are at the funeral home. Is this a memorial, or are you in a casket?" George still is not sure if I know what I am doing, but he tells me he is in a casket. If he says he is cremated or it is a memorial, we will essentially adapt the process to accomplish the same outcome.

"Look all around and tell me what you see." I want George to create *surplus reality*.

George looks around, points to the far wall, and tells me, "The casket is over there." It is important that he experience this scene in the present and as realistically as possible, so I ask him to tell me about size, color, texture, any smell, and even what he hears. A good rule of thumb is to ask the client to tell you what he or she experiences through all of the five senses (sight, touch, taste, smell, and sound).

George tells me that the carpet is tan; the ceiling is off-white, and there is indirect lighting. He sees draped windows on one side of the room and says the room smells like flowers. He says it is quiet and he knows most of the people attending the funeral. Notice that I keep everything in the *present*. He must feel that he is here in the funeral parlor so he will step into that *third dimension*. I want him to step across the frame and into the picture.

Stop the client if you hear, "I guess there would be a wall with windows, etc." I do not want the client to pretend. I want him to experience the scene. That is why I do not say "pretend you are dead" or "pretend" anything. I delete *pretend* from my vocabulary.

The next step is the most critical. We are in the *action phase*. He must *reverse roles* with himself in the casket just created by three chairs set side by side. George lies down on the chairs faceup with his arms folded across his chest. Deceased George must become present in the scene. I bring the deceased George into the present by having a brief interview to learn about his perceptions of life after death.

I begin with noninvasive peripheral questions and keep them simple. Examples: "What is your name?" "How old are you?" "When did you die?" "What do you miss most?" "Who misses you most?" "If you could come back to life, what one thing would you change?" I find it interesting that he says, "Be more assertive."

I say, "I am going to ask you to talk to George in a minute because he needs your advice as he searches for more meaning to his life. I think you are the only person who can help."

I ask him to *reverse roles*. George moves from the "casket" and stands next to it, viewing the deceased George where he can ask the most troublesome questions. Deceased George has become present in the session.

I say, "Tell George in the casket about your search for meaning." I bring the session back to the issue identified when we began. George is empowered to tell himself (George in the casket) about his search.

Looking down at the casket, George says, "I have acquired all kinds of things, and I am satisfied with my accomplishments, but I do not feel fulfilled. I am still trying to find meaning to my existence." George is able to talk to himself in the casket because we took the time to bring the deceased George into the present moment. George is experiencing everything in the *here and now*.

I say, "When you *reverse roles* with yourself in the casket, you will experience an inner wisdom that eludes you now. You will have answers to the difficult questions. Please *reverse roles* with yourself in the casket." Note that I plant the idea of wisdom in George's mind. It is difficult for him to ignore my suggestion.

George reverses roles and becomes the deceased George. I say to George in the casket, "Before you died, you were preoccupied with a search for meaning to your life. Your view of life is much different now and perhaps filled with wisdom. Please give George your guidance."

George, in the casket, looks up at George and says, "George, you need to risk more. You are timid and reluctant to get involved in life. If you are serious about your search, start getting involved in things that are risky but important to you!"

I am somewhat surprised by his insight. Perhaps talking aloud helps him see things more clearly. I say, "*Reverse roles.*" I then say, "You may talk to him about that if you wish."

George stands up and looks at the casket (chairs) and ponders for a moment. He says, "I think I knew that, and I have thought of getting involved. Perhaps I can get involved with the Brothers and Sisters projects, but I have not done it because I don't think I have anything to offer. Maybe I should try because I want to make a difference. Yeah, that might be a way to begin my search."

I ask George standing by the casket to *reverse roles*. Looking down at him, I say, "Share helpful suggestions with the living George. Confront him with his own reality." I want more interaction.

George in the casket says, "This time, you will need to follow through. You have always thought that giving of yourself will award meaning to your life, but in the end you always back out. You need to be different this time."

George reverses roles, stands, and says, "I think I have always looked for some kind of sign to nudge me into action. I really know it is up to me, so I think I need to risk and do something with or without a prophetic sign."

George is in his own role, so I decide to end the drama for today and assess what has been learned. We fold the chairs and put them away.

I ask, "Tell me what you have learned." (This is as close as we get to the sharing phase of the drama.)

George says, "I learned that maybe my concern is not terribly difficult to address. I just have to get off my duff and do something."

"When do you think you will do it?"

"Sometime next week."

We make an appointment for next week to discuss the progress.

It is obvious that interaction between roles is accomplished by reversing roles as many times as necessary. For example, when the client asks a question, immediately reverse roles so the client can answer. The number of reversals will depend on how often the client gets stuck and needs the reversal or because the director can see value in a reversal. The director must trace the dialogue and decide where it is headed. The director is the producer of the drama and can ensure that it moves to a productive end.

When I bring the session to a close, I do three important things. First, I make sure the client is back to the present in his own ego state in my office. I avoid leaving the client in the role of the absent person or other ego state. Second, I consider where I started the drama so we can assess the progress of the session. Third, we agree on a plan of action.

This chapter should give you an idea of how to initiate psychodrama in your office with one client. You must have the conviction that the client has the power to discover answers. I have found that clients will listen to their own advice with more conviction than when listening to my advice. It is easy and compelling for the *director* to pontificate, but it is often a weak response to urgent quests.

By the way, George came back two more times. He carried out his conscious decision to become involved with the Brothers and Sisters. He eventually joined a service club that gave him the reinforcement of a group to continue on his journey.

CHAPTER FIVE

SEXUAL ABUSE

This case study demonstrates how to use psychodrama à deux with issues of sexual abuse. In this case, the marriage is suffering. I will introduce the use of a *soliloquy* to facilitate a conversation between the victim and her father. You will see how I use a dry-erase board to help visualize priorities and focus the session.

Emily was sexually abused from approximately ages eight to twelve by her father. Her sleep is frequently interrupted by a recurring nightmare of trying to escape from her father but feeling paralyzed to do so. Her husband of five years has convinced her to get professional help. She is twenty-five years old, married, and has a three-year-old daughter named Rachael.

She cautiously enters the office for our first appointment. I usher her to a chair and say, "Good afternoon, Emily." She carefully gathers her skirt around her and takes a seat across from me. She looks down at her tightly folded hands.

I ask, "Is this the first time you have come to a counselor?"

"Yes, but I'm not sure what I should talk about."

"Start with how you feel right now." Starting in the present moment sets a tone that we are here to examine feelings in this moment rather than begin digging into history. Regardless of the counseling method I use, I want to understand my client's perception of reality in the moment.

She says, "I usually keep my feelings hidden, so to be here is a little frightening."

I say, "First, Emily, we only talk about things in your life that concern you. Second, whatever we talk about in this room stays here. I will break confidentiality only if there is potential danger to you or someone else."

—

She says, "Well, my husband thinks that I should talk about my nightmares."

"On a scale of 1 to 10, with 10 giving the nightmares your greatest concern, what number do *you* give to these nightmares?" I also write *nightmares* on a dry-erase board. She assigns nightmares a weight of 8. I often use the board because it is helpful to visual learners as well as in promoting concentration and recall.

I underline *nightmares*, followed by the number 8. I then draw another line under *nightmares* and ask, "What else should we put on the list of concerns?"

She seems more relaxed and is very intent on looking at the potential list. I wait. She says, "Relationships." So I write it on the board, asking what number I should give to *relationships*. She hesitates but says, "I think it is as high as the nightmares." She finds it is easier to name her feelings when she is concentrating on the board. In this early stage of counseling, it is helpful for a client to simply join me as we both study the board because we are joined on this journey and threat is reduced. The brief silence is less deafening to her. As can be seen, this is still part of the *warm-up*.

I ask, "*Could it be* that the two concerns are connected in some way?" I often use the phrase "could it be" because a timid client finds the question easy to answer. "Are the two connected?" is also a logical question but slightly more direct.

She deliberates, staring at the board without looking at me. "Yes, I think they are connected. I need to talk about my marriage. We don't fight, but we don't seem to be very close—at least not like we used to be."

"Can you tell me more about that?"

"Tom is very kind, but we don't seem as close as we once did."

I ask, "Is it like two people occupying the same house but not sharing their lives together?" My question is an effort to define what she means by *close*.

She says, "In a way, yes, but we talk about Rachael and surface things. It isn't fair to complain because I am never mistreated. It's just that I need to feel cared for."

"Tell me more about your need to be cared for."

"I have always wanted to be protected and cared for, but I am uncomfortable asking for it. That's why I can't blame others. I don't communicate my needs very well."

We continue while she gives more examples of this concern. She avoids discussion of her father or much about her childhood experiences. We are still *warming up* to the real issues.

I ask, "May I tell you what I know so far and what we can do in our sessions together? [She nods her head.] I know that this has been a brave thing for you to come here today. I respect that. I know that the nightmares are troublesome, and they frighten you. I also know that you are frightened in a different way for your marriage and that you want to become more comfortable expressing your needs." She nods her head in agreement but this time looking at me with anticipation. "When we get together next week, we will talk more, but in the meantime, I want you to get a spiral notebook and record other feelings that come to mind." Assignments are an important part of counseling because the client can examine and share insights.

This *warm-up* session accomplishes two things. First, Emily needs to feel safe, so I move slowly. Second, I need information from Emily in order to know how to move to the *action* phase of our work together.

We meet at the same time the following week. She brings her notebook and somewhat apologetically says she did not write very much. As I scan the pages, she says, "I think I have always had problems trusting Tom." I take my marker and write *trust* at the top of the dry-erase board and say, "Help me understand what trust means to you?"

She contemplates the word. "I think I mean Tom isn't there when I need him. I can't find the words, but I often feel alone."

Persistent feelings usually are fixed there early in life, so my next question is deliberately intended to move her to another level. I ask, "Where and when have you felt this way early in your life?" If I find the roots, they may be exposed, and Emily might become free of their grip.

The next phrase is significant. "*I felt the same way with my father. I never trusted him. He was never what he seemed to be.*"

I ask, "Did that frighten you?" I use the word *frightened* because it has a softer tone than, for example, "He deceived you."

"Yes!"

"What frightened you the most?"

"When he touched me." We are now approaching the protected and complex feelings that she has learned explicitly or implicitly not to share. She very carefully risks revealing her guarded feelings. I remind myself that *I am not here to gather evidence to convict the father. I am here to help her unearth buried experiences.* Even Emily does not know what has been concealed.

I turn away from the erase board and, with obvious concern, say, "Please tell me more so I can understand." It does not take a mental giant to know what happened with her father, but pacing is part of the art of counseling. If I leap forward too quickly, I can easily lose her.

"Well, when I was a little girl, my dad touched me inappropriately. When I sat on his lap, he put his hands in wrong places. It never felt right, but I wanted his affection. Now, when I read magazine articles by people who say they were sexually abused, I see myself." The dreadful words have been said aloud—*sexually abused.*

I say something that is very Rogerian, "You were confused because you wanted his affection, but at the same time, it did not seem right. How do you think those feelings still affect your life?" At this point, dwelling on historical specifics of the abuse is not essential. I want to stay in the present. I want to understand *how the past impacts the present.*

Emily continues, "I feel confused when Tom shows me affection. Sometimes I am not sure how to respond. Then Tom pulls away, and I feel guilty."

I say, "Emily, there are some things that you and Tom need to talk about." We will work through issues with her father later. We must stay in the present and deal with the past when she is ready.

I say to Emily, "We need to bring Tom to this session so you and he can talk." I open two of my folding chairs and place them face-to-face. I ask Emily to sit in one of them.

I say, "Emily, it is vital that Tom join us because you need to explain your feelings to him. But before you say anything, I want you to reverse roles with Tom so I can get acquainted with him. He is joining us through you. Please sit in one of the chairs. Be Tom."

Reversing roles is absolutely essential. *I must interview the absent person so he becomes present here and now.* He is my source of information. A reminder, I do not tell Emily to *pretend* that Tom is present. If I say, "Imagine that Tom is here," the pretense will taint the session and contaminate my efforts to move her into surplus reality where her spontaneity and creativity open new windows through which to see herself in the present and the past.

Emily now becomes Tom, and I ask, "Tom, how old are you?" I follow that question with, "Tom, how long have you been married to Emily?" Then I ask, "Tom, tell me about your marriage to Emily." I proceed with, "Tom, you have suggested that Emily go for counseling. Why?"

There are two things to note. First, I deliberately use Tom's name at the beginning of each question. Remember, it is Emily to whom I am speaking; therefore, using Tom's name imprints that I am talking to Tom and that the answers are from Tom. The second thing to remember, as mentioned before, is that questions move from the periphery to the center. That is, from least intrusive questions to the edge of her comfort zone.

Tom, through Emily, says that he is twenty-seven; that they have been married for five years; and that he is concerned about her nightmares. He continues, "I think our marriage is good. We don't fight often, but in the last couple of years, we don't talk much either. I want to know why we are not as close as we used to be."

I want the question to hang in the air as a stimulus to the dialogue between Emily and Tom. I am impressed by the penetrating nature of questions from an absent person! I realize, of course, it is the client who is talking; but while she is in surplus reality, it is Tom talking phenomenologically through Emily.

I ask her to reveres roles. Physically moving to the other chair is important because the action of moving makes the absent person remain real and in the present.

I turn to her and say, "Tom just asked why the two of you don't seem to be close anymore. He is right here, so please tell him why." She turns to the empty chair and thinks for a moment.

Emily says, "Except for Rachael, we don't seem to have anything in common anymore."

I say, "Tell him about your nightmares." Tom needs to know how the dreams connect to her father because I suspect she has never told Tom about her dad's behavior.

She looks at Tom and says, "You know I don't like being around my dad, and I never leave Rachael alone with him. When I wake up screaming, it's because I am dreaming that I cannot escape from Dad. He was horrible to me, and I fear for Rachael." Tears well up in her eyes.

I sit in silence with her. I place the drama on pause to ask a cognitive question because at that moment it is important to ask, "How much does Tom know?"

"He knows Dad had wandering hands, but he does not know that Dad came to my bed at night. I am afraid to tell him."

I say, "Tom is not physically here, so you can safely tell him your story." Surplus reality protects her from recriminations. The tele between us also gives her courage.

Emily turns her attention to the empty chair and says, "Tom, I haven't told you the whole story about Dad. You know that he was inappropriate with me, but I've never told you he came to my room at night. He frightened me. At first he just held me, and I thought that was all right. But soon he started to make me do things to him. When he was finished, he left me and went back to bed. I felt terribly ashamed and dirty. He told me never to tell Mom. He made me do that at least once a week for over three years. Can you ever forgive me, Tom?"

I tell her to reverse roles. In the role of Tom without my prompting, she says, "You were a child! He was your father. What could you do? I feel so bad that you still carry this yourself. It was not your fault! You are my wife. I love you."

I ask her to reverse roles. (*A reminder—never stop with your client in the role of the absent person.*) She moves to her chair and says, "I knew that is how you would feel. You are a good man. You are good to me. I am sorry, but I have been too frightened to share that experience with you or anyone. I need your help to get through this."

There is about ten minutes left in the session, but we need a response from Tom. I ask her to reverse roles with Tom one more time. She does and says, "We will get through this together!"

She moves back to her position, and I ask that she put the chairs away.

We move to the *sharing phase*. I ask, "What did you learn today?"

Emily says, "I think I have learned that I need to tell Tom what happened."

I assign her to continue the journal and also to find a time when she can confide this part of her life with Tom at home.

I note in her chart that her father needs to be psychodramatically confronted, perhaps during the next session. I believe encounters between victims and perpetrators are most often best done psychodramatically rather than face-to-face. I realize this runs counter to the practice of some therapists who believe a client should confront the perpetrator in person. I have concluded after close to forty years of counseling that the perpetrator most often defends his actions and the victim comes away angry and disillusioned with no more closure than when she or he began. Perpetrators often have a narcissistic personality disorder that strips them of empathy and accepting personal responsibility.

At the beginning of the next session, Emily says, "I think I need to deal with some of the stuff about my father. I have put off confronting him far too long. He needs to know how badly he affected me." Emily finds role-reversal techniques helpful and is anxious for an opportunity to confront her father.

I say, "Before we jump into that, can you tell me what happened with your assignment?" *I deliberately delay the dramatic confrontation with the father because I am concerned she will leap to an abreactive catharsis without adequate warm-up.* That is, she may experience a release of repressed emotions that may feel good but may serve little more. I want the encounter with her father to feel authentic, and I want her to experience an *integrative catharsis* through which she may integrate her experiences and emotions and discover a new *conserve*. That is, eventually form a tolerable perception of her father.

Emily tells me, "When Tom and I were alone, I talked to him pretty much the same way I did in our last session. I held my breath, waiting for him to say something. Then he said he suspected that Dad had treated me badly but what happened does not change the love he has for me. I feel so much closer to him now because that secret is in the open and not between us."

I ask, "What do both of you need to do so you can build on this?"

"Keep talking openly to each other. I need to stop guessing what he thinks and just ask."

"When you came today, you said you need to confront your father. Apparently you have been thinking about this since we last met. What do you need to say to him?"

"I'm not sure!"

I tell Emily that some people find it helpful to do a *soliloquy*. I say, "A soliloquy is simply thinking aloud. All of us talk to ourselves in an effort to understand ourselves or someone else. For example, after I meet an important person, I might preview what to say. I might say to myself, 'I want to ask intelligent questions about his life.' Or, I might say to myself, 'I don't want to talk too much.' The point is, Emily, I want you to let your mind wander, but put words aloud to your thoughts and let me eavesdrop."

"That feels a little embarrassing."

I say, "Free your mind, and let me hear your thoughts concerning a talk with your dad."

"How do you want me to say it?"

"Let me give you an example of what is going on in my mind right now. *I wonder if there is a better way for me to explain this to Emily. I think if she can say her thoughts aloud, she might find a way to begin with her father. I want to help her, but I can't tell her what to say. I feel frustrated.*" I ask, "Does that help you, Emily?"

"Yes. I will try. *I really want to hurt him like he hurt me. But I am not like that. But he needs to know what pain he caused. Maybe I need to just talk from my heart—as if my heart is a concern to him. He is such an asshole for what he did!*"

"Emily, is your mind more focused after listening to your own comments?"

"It helped hearing myself. What do I do now?"

I respond, "I want you to select a place where a talk with your father can take place." (scene setting)

"I want to talk to him in my living room. That way I am in control, and when we are finished, he can go home."

"All right, we will go there. When does this take place?"

Emily decides to talk to her father in the morning after Rachael leaves for school and Tom is at work.

I say, "Describe your living room so that I can see it in my mind."

She tells me, "It is a typical-sized living room, probably twelve by fourteen feet, with the door over there and a large window over here looking out on the front lawn and the street. The couch is near that wall, and two recliners are across from it. No, the couch and chairs are over there. There are pictures on these walls and an arrangement of flowers on the small coffee table by the couch. The floor is hardwood, with an area rug near the middle. The walls are light blue, and the ceiling is off-white. I can faintly smell the bacon from breakfast because the kitchen is just around the corner. It is quiet except for the ticking of the clock near the door." The *scene setting* rolled from her mind in an even, uninterrupted stream. Nevertheless, she walks around the office, studying the room as it emerges in her mind's eye. She pauses and makes corrections.

I say, "Stand in the center of your living room and look around. Does it feel familiar? Are you there?" She looks around and nods her head.

"Do you want your father to come in through the door, or can he simply be placed in the room?"

"I don't need the doorbell. He can just be here."

"Where?"

"In that recliner, but it is not reclined."

I say, "Please reverse roles with him." She sits in the recliner (represented by a folding chair she has placed in the living room along with other props).

I interview the father. "I know that you are Emily's father, but I do not know your name."

"My name is John."

I now begin to introduce questions about Emily. "John, describe Emily as a child."

He says, "She was always a good girl. She never gave us any trouble."

"Do you remember going to her room at night to maybe tuck her in?"

"Sure. Just like most fathers who tell their daughters good night."

"Do you remember anything else when you checked in on her at night?"

"No, I hardly ever remember checking in on her at night."

I say, "Well, John, Emily is going to help you remember." I ask Emily to reverse roles.

She moves from being John to the chair across from him. At this point, I take a small nylon rope (about a half inch in diameter) and stretch it between the two chairs. I say, "Emily, this is the parent/child *boundary* that should have always been there. It will remain there. Your father no longer is allowed to cross it." A counselor acquires an array of props to help the dramatization. I have found a six-foot, half-inch nylon rope useful in many situations—especially defining boundaries.

I continue, "Emily, your father's memory needs some help. Tell him what he did to you and the effect it still has on you. You are in control and safe here, so take your time. You have the power and the strength to say whatever you wish, and the boundary is there to stay."

She looks at the chair and down at the rope, hesitates for a moment to gather her thoughts, and then says, "I'm sorry, I just cannot do it!"

I get another chair and place it behind and a little to the right of the chair she just occupied and from which she was unable to talk to her dad. I explain to Emily, "This chair represents your *double*. It is you, but different because this double of you has been given courage to talk to Father. Please stand here beside me to look at the two women. Look at the first chair of Emily. What one word describes her?"

Emily says, "Coward."

I ask, "What does she look like?"

"She is looking down at her lap, afraid to look at her dad."

I say, "Tell me what you see that is different about the Emily who is doubling for you."

Emily says, "She is looking at Dad. I see anger in her eyes. She is sitting straight and looks strong."

I tell Emily, "Sit in the chair of the double. You know how she looks, and you see the determination. I want to hear from that double. There is your dad."

Emily in the role of *double* says, "Dad, I don't care if you remember or not. The truth is you came to my room when I was just a little girl and you made me do despicable things to you. You had no right to do that. I was a helpless child and could not stop you—I was afraid, so I always did what you wanted!"

She continues, "You know something? You were the helpless bastard. You used other people, and you still do! I want you out of my head! I want you out of my marriage with Tom. He is nothing like you. He is a man with integrity. But you don't know anything about that, do you! I don't hate you. I feel sorry for you. You are pathetic!"

Her anger turns to tears. She is sobbing into her hands.

Her reaction is a small sample of an abreaction because she has brought some unconscious feeling to a conscious level. An abreaction can reflect an extreme emotional reaction that can connect the client to another moment or place. (That is why great care must be taken when sensitive and painful experiences are exposed.)

In spite of the emotional drain, she needs to move to the first Emily. We no longer need a double. I am silent for a moment to assess her needs. I then tell her to return to the front chair. Only after she returns to the primary Emily do I ask her to *reverse roles* with her father.

I say to John, "You heard every word Emily said, and you know she tells the truth. Is there anything you can say that might help her?"

John looks down and says, "You are right, Emily. I could not stop myself. I am sorry."

I wait, but it seems that is all Emily is going to say as John. So I intervene by telling John, "You have let Emily feel guilty for all these years. You have an obligation to say something to help her." As the therapist/director, I have the obligation to enhance the drama with questions or even statements that capture the precision of an issue. In a way, I am indirectly functioning as an auxiliary. Perhaps I am in the role of his conscience. The only caveat is that I must not derail the drama by bringing an unrelated issue to the session. In other words, I can say the word or ask the question that exposes the unacknowledged issue.

Emily, still in the role of John, says, "Emily, there is nothing you did that made me do it. It was just me. I don't expect you to understand. You didn't do anything. I am sorry."

I ask her to reverse to her own role to determine if she needs to say anything else to him. She says to me, the director, "Maybe someday I can forgive him, but not yet."

"Do you want to tell him?"

"No, not now. I am out of patience with him today. I just want him to leave."

She tells John to leave. I get up and remove the chair in which John sat, pick up the rope, turn to Emily, and ask, "Tell me what you are feeling right now." This question keeps us in the present and also focuses on the *impact of the action*.

Emily says, "I have a feeling of relief. Maybe I feel a little stronger. He really was a bastard, but I can't ignore that he is my father."

"You need not destroy whatever relationship you have with your father. No one is saying you need to hate him. Nevertheless, you need to take back your power and let him own his disgrace." She must validate herself and internalize an image of her father painted in a different shade.

We are almost out of time for this session. I ask that she come back next week and that she keep journaling.

I say, "Someday it may be possible to forgive him. I suspect your personal freedom is connected to forgiving." It is acceptable to plant the seed of forgiveness.

We meet for six consecutive weeks and after that, every six weeks. Our sessions terminate one year after they begin. During the year that I see her, Emily does several more three-dimensional encounters with her father to deal with residual anger and guilt.

At times the specificity of the abuse (*the abreaction*) generated intense fear and distress. On two additional occasions we use more than one chair to *double* for Emily—giving her more physical distance and a buffer from her father and the courage to disengage from his disabling irrational treatment. I distance Emily from her father with as many empty chairs as necessary. I used a *soliloquy* again when I asked Emily to sit in the closest chair. I moved her to the second chair and did the same thing. Finally, in the third chair, the *soliloquy* reflected a comfort that allowed her to verbalize her father's behavior with more specificity.

In order to let go of the pain and anger, the final task is forgiving her father. Again, she uses one chair to distance herself from her father. She chooses to forgive him and recognize him as a flawed human being, but she does not forgive his behavior. She cannot forgive what he did to her. It is a difficult and lengthy task, but the infectious poison of hate is neutralized.

Eventually, she has a significant nurturing and healing psychodramatic encounter with her severely injured "inner child." She held a rag doll to concretize the experience. Healing the inner child is very important part of counseling a victim because, contrary to some popular opinion, time does not heal all wounds. That eight-year-old Emily is still terrified and bewildered. She continues to believe that there was something dreadful she had done to merit such treatment by her father. In this case, the most powerful medicine comes from the adult Emily whose soothing, nurturing presence has the influence to heal the injured soul.

I have kept in contact with Emily over several years. She reports that she and Tom share their feelings and dreams with each other in a way she never imagined. She tells me that they invite her parents to the house occasionally, but her father is never alone with Rachael.

She says, "Even though I will never be close to Dad, his presence does not overpower me. I am disengaged from his parent role, and I am my own person. That imaginary rope is always there!"

I continue to relearn lessons with every client. I relearned from Emily that the human spirit does not die easily. Also, I affirmed that faulty logic and faulty conclusions can be successfully challenged and modified.

Dr. John Nolte published (1990) a comprehensive paper on the use of psychodrama to treat survivors of incest and other kinds of sexual abuse. His paper presents history and rationale for the method and emphasizes that careful judgment must be used during the action. The power of psychodrama becomes evident through his accounts of the method. He underscores the importance of being sensitive to the energy released by the protagonist.

CHAPTER SIX

UNFINISHED BUSINESS

This is a common and uncomplicated case. It is an account of a client whose father unexpectedly dies before there is an opportunity for closure. After a person dies, there is often unfinished business related to the relationship. There are feelings and thoughts left unexpressed. We often are not ready to let go. This case shows the effectiveness of role reversal.

Joe's father died the night before he was to have open-heart surgery. Joe still feels the devastation of the loss. Dr. Horst, Joe's family physician, tells me Joe has consulted a psychiatrist and received a diagnosis of major depressive disorder, single episode. Joe is on a mild antidepressant when he comes to me.

I ask, "Where do you want to begin?" We need to *warm up* to his need for therapy.

Joe says, "Since my dad died, I can't seem to get him off my mind! He and I were very close, and I can't believe he died before I told him how I felt!"

"Tell me more about that," I ask.

"Dad and I cherished our friendship. I think I shared almost everything in my life with him. I know that he felt close to me, but we never talked much about it. I keep going over and over in my mind what I should have said to him that night."

I say, "And now you are full of regret and disappointment."

It is normal to feel grief, guilt, or remorse when someone close to us dies, especially when there is unfinished business. Kubler-Ross (1969) presents a widely accepted model of loss. It is easy to understand that Joe is in a stage of depression, but as Kubler-Ross wrote, he is cycling through more than one stage.

I set up my erase board and ask him to name his feelings. He names *regret*, *sad*, *lonely*, and *guilty*. I ask if these can be arranged in order of importance. Joe takes a moment to consider the answer and says, "Regret goes on the top of the list, with guilt right below it."

I tell Joe, "Since you frequently talked things over with your dad, would it be helpful for you to tell your dad about your feelings?"

In spite of being puzzled by my statement, he answers, "I think so—but he is dead."

"We will use this empty chair to bring your dad here so you can talk to him."

Empty chair is a frequently used Gestalt therapy term. However, I do not consider the chair "empty." Psychodrama creates the presence of the absent person. It will not be an empty chair to the client.

I ask Joe to sit in the chair designated for his dad. I say, "Joe, I want to meet your father."

I continue, "You are Joe's dad. What is your name?" Asking the name of the absent person is a common way to begin a dyadic encounter.

Joe (in the role of his father) says, "My name is Harold."

I continue with questions that provide important data and coincidentally establish Dad's presence in the counseling session. For example, I ask when and how old he was when he died, how many children he had, what he did for a living, etc. Notice that I deliberately frame the questions in past tense because I want Joe to continue facing the reality of his father's death. Questions have been quite factual, but now I ask Dad about his son.

"Harold, tell me about Joe," I say.

"Joe was always a good boy. We worked side by side on the farm. Joe is doing well."

I tell Joe to reverse roles. Joe moves to the other chair and faces his father. I urge him to say whatever is on his mind.

Joe begins to cry and asks, "Why did you have to die before I could talk to you?" Joe's warm-up is complete!

I immediately ask him to reverse roles because a basic rule of psychodrama is that the client answers his own question. I resist a cognitive question like, "What do you think he would say?" That removes him from the time and space he occupies with his father and also changes the affective encounter with his father to a cognitive exchange with me.

After the role reversal, I look at Harold and say, "Joe has just asked why you died before he could talk to you."

Harold turns to Joe and answers, "You knew I had that heart condition. It was worse than any of us thought. I also wish I had more time."

I tell Joe to reverse roles. He is now facing Harold and says, "You are right. We thought the surgery was going to fix everything. I just was not ready. I wanted to tell you how important you were to me. When I was growing up, you were always there to help or give me advice. You always listened to what I had to say when we worked together. I just want you to know you are still living in my heart." Joe breaks down and cries again. It is a liberating catharsis.

After Joe composes himself, I ask that he reverse roles, and I ask, "Harold, what does Joe need to know? You have wisdom to share with Joe." Again, I use the idea of "wisdom figure" to free my client to say things that are important.

Harold says, "You must remember we are separate people. I have lived my life. Now it is your turn to live yours."

I ask Joe to move back to his role and ask if he needs to say anything else to his dad.

He says, "Dad, we both knew how deep our respect and love went. I just want to say another time that I love you."

I wait a moment and ask, "Do you have other things on your mind, or are we finished?"

Joe says, "Yes, we are finished." I remove Harold's chair and ask, "What have you learned, and what are you taking away with you?" (*sharing phase*)

He says, "I learned that he wants me to go on with my life. I guess I had to hear that. I also learned that I can keep his legacy alive through me. I am taking away a peace that I have not felt since he died. I am going to be all right."

We select a follow-up session in two weeks when we can assess his progress.

As you can see, this case is not a complicated set of issues needing to be unraveled from repressed unconscious feelings. It is a clear-cut example of a client needing to confront unfinished business, let go, and get on with his life. The power usually lies within the client waiting to be unleashed. Also, the case study is an example of brief therapy and how one session can make a difference.

CHAPTER SEVEN

DEPRESSION

This case applies action therapy for a high school senior who feels defeated and depressed. You will read about interpsychic and intrapsychic encounters that demonstrate the use of role reversal to deal with other people and with internal struggles. There also is an example of how to use role reversal to look at issues between a client and both parents.

Chuck is a high school senior with several defining characteristics of depression. He has sleepless nights, relatively flat affect, lacks energy, has low self-esteem, and poor concentration. He is socially withdrawn.

I work with Chuck in consultation with his psychiatrist whose diagnosis of Chuck is adjustment disorder with depressed mood. Chuck is taking an antidepressant. His psychiatrist indicates that Chuck has responded positively to the medication but has issues that continue to trigger mood swings. A bipolar disorder has been ruled out.

He arrives for our first session but seems uneasy. I say, "Can you tell me what you are feeling right now?" I focus on the present moment (*warm-up*).

Chuck answers, "I guess being here makes me uncomfortable. I don't know what I'm supposed to do. Dr. Stevens, the psychiatrist, asked me a few questions, gave me a prescription, and I left. I know I'm supposed to talk, but I don't know what to say."

"Tell me what a typical day is like for you." (*More warm-up.*)

"This is my senior year, so I spend all day at school. My older brother graduated last year and is in college. School is easy for him. After school, I work at the lumberyard until about six in the evening, then I go home and do homework."

I want to know how his depression is affecting his life, so I ask, "What is it like when you have severe depression?"

"I have trouble just getting out of bed. I don't feel like doing anything. Mom and Dad get all pissed off because I don't talk to them. I just want to be left alone."

I set up the erase board. We need to give a weight or value to the things he is carrying around. I wonder if a metaphor may depict his state of mind. I draw a stick figure with its back bent over as if weighted down with something. It looks like a Kokopelli, a drawing commonly seen in Southwestern art.

"Is this stick man like you? Are you bent over carrying the weight of something?"

He studies it and nods his head. We wait. Finally, Chuck says, "I will never measure up. People keep expecting things of me, but I just can't be what they want."

I ask, "Does it feel heavy?" He nods.

I draw a box on the stick man's back and ask, "Can you name the things on your back that feel heavy?"

With sagging shoulders and some sorrow in his face, he says, "Be somebody. Get good grades. Make some friends. Be like your brother." I write them on the board.

We have a place to begin. I ask, "Can you pick the heaviest one?" He points to "Be somebody" and "Be like your brother."

William Glasser frames *depression* as a verb suggesting that we choose to depress because depressing controls anger (1984, 49). I look for signs of anger at self or others when I ask, "How did they get on your back?"

Chuck says, "I don't know. Maybe they have always been there. There is a part of me that hates who I am, but there is a small part of me that won't give up."

When I hear a client present a clear dichotomy of feelings like "one *part* of me feels this way while the other *part* of me feels that way," I decide that an intrapsychic encounter may clarify the inner conflicts. I want Chuck to understand his self-hate as well as the courage that keeps him going. I know he is angry with other people, but I choose to delay that encounter until later.

My first objective or goal of the session is to get a sense of the potency of the two parts of his personal assessment. So I open three folding chairs. One chair is for the Chuck present with me in the office. The second chair is the part of him identified as "I hate myself." The third chair is the part of him identified as "I won't give up."

I ask him to pick the chair that is the "complete" Chuck present with me today and place it against the far wall. I then ask that he select the chair that is labeled "I hate myself" and show me how close it is to the "complete" Chuck. I then tell him to take the last chair labeled "I won't give up" and to show me how close it is to the "complete" Chuck with me. This is an elementary task that empowers him to *concretize* his feelings. Placement of the chairs shows which part of his consciousness is most in control. The arrangement of the chairs shows that the "I hate myself" part sits almost on top of Chuck and "I won't give up" part is almost against the opposite wall.

This powerful picture suggests he has almost abandoned hope. I stand so the arrangement of the chairs is clearly in perspective and ask Chuck to stand next to me and observe. I ask, "What do you see?"

Chuck says, "I see that I am giving up. I have a pretty low opinion of myself."

I ask, "Are you angry?"

He says, "Yes. I am disgusted that I don't measure up to what anyone expects!"

Chuck must now give a voice to these parts. I ask him to be the part that sits far away. He walks across the room and sits in the "I won't give up" chair.

I say to Chuck as he sits in the chair, "Explain to Chuck over by the wall what part of him you are." Whenever I do an intrapsychic or interpsychic encounter, I begin with an interview. I want the client to separate the psychic parts from the complete personality. This "internal" dialogue is often difficult for the client. There is a tendency for the client's "parts" to dialogue with the therapist. Two very important things are accomplished, however. First, the interview anchors the feelings firmly to the empty chair. Second, valuable information is collected from the client.

He answers, "I am the weak little voice in Chuck's head that won't give up." The comment is addressed to me, the therapist. I interrupt him and remind him to say these things to the Chuck sitting near the far wall, not to me.

"I keep telling you that things will get better. I encourage you to keep trying. But I know you don't listen to me very often, but I don't know what else to tell you."

I say to the hopeful part of Chuck, "Show Chuck how loud you are."

I see him look down and hear a faint, "Chuck, listen to me." Clients never cease to amaze me. Chuck wants me to understand what is going on inside his head. He deliberately depicts that part of himself as powerless and impotent.

I ask, "Is that usually how weak you sound to Chuck?"

"Yes. Sometimes Chuck doesn't even hear me!"

I choose to do nothing more with this part at this time. I ask him to sit in the "I hate myself" chair. I wonder what will come from this part of Chuck because this part is potentially destructive and seems to be in control.

I say, "Explain to Chuck what role you play."

He answers, "I am the voice that you hear most of the time. You are worthless, especially when you get too confident and self-centered. You need to know that you will never measure up. I sometimes try to get you to just give up, but you are too pigheaded. You keep trying even when you know it won't be good enough."

I ask, "Show Chuck how loud you are."

He almost yells at the top his voice, "Chuck, you are a stupid idiot, why don't you just give up?"

I look at my watch and see that we have twelve minutes left in the session. I need to bring Chuck down from this level of intensity and tie things together. I tell Chuck to sit in the chair that represents the "complete" Chuck present with me today.

I say, "Just sit and recall what you heard from the two parts of yourself today. What will you do with this information?" I am willing to trust Chuck to be thoughtful with this information because he has made it clear that he is resisting the destructive voice. Nevertheless, I formulate in my mind an agreement of self-care if it becomes necessary.

Chuck says, "I don't like that part of me [pointing to the destructive part]. He wants control of me, and he frightens me. I want to listen to that one over there by the wall."

"That is the hopeful part of you. Are you ready to try listening to him?"

"I think I *need* to listen to him," says Chuck.

I make an appointment for the same time next week and give him an assignment to write a paragraph or two about what he learned today and list the times he hears the hopeful voice inside his head. He leaves, and I think I see his shoulders just a little higher, or perhaps I want to see it.

The following Friday, Chuck is on time for our second session. I consult my notes. They suggest I start this session with a question concerning his follow-through on the assignment. I say, "Did you think about what you learned from the last session?" (*Warm-up.*)

"I learned that I am pretty hard on myself."

I ask, "Do you need to be hard on yourself?

"I don't know."

"Where do you think the critical voices are coming from?" I ask. I know I am pushing Chuck, but one of his earlier comments about his brother is lingering in my mind. Where does the brother fit into the picture, and how does Chuck perceive his home experiences? What is his reality? Where does he need to go, and what does he need to do in order to adjust the picture (the conserve) he has in his head? To borrow from Glasser's reality therapy, what pictures from his "album" are being used to satisfy his needs?

Chuck says, "I suppose they are coming from my family experiences, but I can't blame my family for the way I am. There is something wrong with *me*—there always has been."

Resisting an impulse to encourage him to "feel better," I say, "What do you think is wrong with you?"

Chuck stares down at his folded hands and says, "I am a disappointment to Mom and Dad. They don't have to say it—I just know. I don't fit in. I never did. I am alone most of the time."

"How do you know these things?"

"It has been obvious most of my life. My brother, Eric, never has any trouble making friends. I need to be more like him, but I don't know how. It is wrong to be jealous, but I am. We would all be better off if I had not been born."

"What have you told your parents or Eric about how you feel?" I ask.

"I just figure they know. We don't talk about how we feel."

Discussion so far has been *warm-up* for this session.

I say, "I suggest that you need to tell them. They know you are depressed, but it seems you are unable to explain it to them. You need to experience talking to them. I want you to create a time and place to talk. We will bring them here through your mind. I will help you take on this new role."

I bring out three folding chairs—one for Chuck and two for his parents. When I met Chuck last week, he did an *intrapsychic encounter* to experience his internal struggle. Today I want him to do an *interpsychic encounter* with his parents. I direct an interpsychic encounter more elaborately than I do an intrapsychic encounter. The client creates the time and space in which the interactive dialogue takes place. We take time to set the scene. Time and space must feel real to him. I want him to be in surplus reality.

To set the scene, I ask, "Where does this talk with your parents take place?" I keep him in the present and avoid asking, "Where *will* this take place?"

Chuck says, "In the backyard of our house."

I tell him to describe the place so I can feel myself there also.

"There are lawn chairs where I often sit to think and sometimes study."

I ask him to tell me what else he sees.

"I see an oak tree that shades the chairs. I see the neighbor's wooden fence over there and the back of the house over there. The alley is there, and the yard of our other neighbor is there. The lawn is mowed because I just mowed it. I can smell it. The sky is clear. I can hear a bird or two."

I ask what time of day it is.

"It is about four in the afternoon."

I tell him to place two chairs next to each other and a single chair across from them. He does. Then I say, "Sit in one of those two chairs and be your dad." He sits in the chair to the right of his mother.

I ask, "What is your name?"

He tells me his name is James. He says he has two children, one in college and one a senior in high school.

I say, "Of course you know that your son Chuck is seeing me for counseling. What do you think is his problem?" I ask this to see how Chuck perceives his father's opinion of his depression.

Chuck (as James) tells me, "Chuck is a loner. You know how some people see the glass as half empty—well, Chuck is one of them. We have tried to understand, but I guess we don't. All of us have ups and downs. Most of us snap out of it. I guess Chuck can't."

I ask James, "How are your two boys the same and different?"

"They never have been the same. We never expected Chuck to be able to compete with Eric. Eric was gifted from the day he was born. Nobody could measure up to Eric—even his classmates."

I need to hear from the mother, so I remove Chuck from the role of father and move him back to his own role. I tell him to just look at his father for a few seconds and think of what his father has said. *It is important that a client move back to his own role before he assumes another role.*

I say, "Your mother is beside your dad. Please reverse roles with her." He does.

I interview Mother. I ask her name and what she wants to add to her husband's comments.

(Chuck says in the role of Mother) "My name is Helen, and I am worried sick about Chuck. I try to get him to talk to me, but it never seems to work. He is so withdrawn and quiet. I try my best."

I ask Chuck to reverse roles and sit in the chair facing the parents. I tell him, "You need to tell your parents about your struggle. They need to hear the explanation of fears and resentments that have been around for years."

"I don't know if I can."

"Chuck, it is very important that you tell them that you have anger, and they need to know that depression is painful and that often life seems hopeless. Since you have never done it, I am going to put another chair behind your chair. In it will sit a Chuck who has the courage to say whatever is on his mind. Do you understand? He is a Chuck who can do that. We are going to call him your *double*. He is like you in every way except he is fearless!"

The reader recognizes this technique as *doubling*. Notice, I do not become an auxiliary and serve as the double. I use guided imagery and suggestion to accomplish doubling. I tell Chuck, "Stand with me here. Look at the two Chucks. One is afraid and one is bold. Picture them. See the difference. When you are ready, stand in front of the second chair."

Chuck moves to the second chair. The second "chair" is a high stool to symbolize power. Chuck stands in front of the stool.

Finally, Chuck says, "I want both of you to listen to me. Right now I don't see much in my life to live for. I don't know how to climb out of this. I just know I feel really angry, and I'm not sure why. I have been angry for years. I'm angry because I never ever measured up. I have never been good enough. Sometimes I hate myself. Eric has always been the shining boy. He did everything right. I hate him for what he got that I didn't get even though he never treated me badly. Damn it all! I am a person too!" Chuck places his hands over his eyes and shakes his head.

He is obviously getting in touch with some repressed anger. I don't want him to close up again, so while he is still warmed up, I decide to have him reverse roles with his dad. I choose his dad because I believe Chuck's strongest feelings are connected to his father.

I say, "Reverse roles with your dad."

Chuck moves to his father's chair. I look at Chuck in the role of Dad and say, "James, you heard what Chuck just said. He feels hopeless and angry. He needs to hear from you."

In the role of Dad, Chuck says, "Chuck, you never gave us any trouble. I always thought you were just quiet and wanted to be alone. It wasn't until just lately I found out that you are depressed. I don't know much about depression. I just know I didn't mean to treat you different. I just thought that's the way you are. I am sorry. I don't know what I'm supposed to do."

Chuck reverses roles but still, interestingly, chooses the high chair and sits down. He tells his dad, "All I need to know is you care and that my life means something to you. Is that so hard?"

I say, "Reverse roles with Dad."

In the role of his dad, I hear, "Chuck, I don't want to make excuses, but when you were born, I was on the road a lot. I was trying to make a living, so when I was home, I was tired. You need to know I cared, but you never seemed to need attention, and Eric just naturally got it. I don't travel so much anymore, but now you are about ready to leave home. I do not know what to do that would make you feel better."

Chuck reverses into his own role but this time takes the low chair. "Can you give your dad an idea how he can help you?" I ask.

Chuck says to his father, "We cannot change the past. We don't even know each other. I think we need to get acquainted before I go away to college or whatever. That goes for you too, Mom."

We still have a few minutes left in the session, so I ask Chuck to reverse roles with his mother.

I say, "Helen, you've heard all this. Do you have an idea what Chuck and his dad might do?"

She answers without much hesitation, "Maybe they need to do something together."

I tell Chuck to reverse to his own role. I decide to let Chuck see the action through a "*mirror*." I tell Chuck to step out of his role and stand next to me so he sees the three empty chairs. They resemble the points of a triangle. He and I stand together and view the scene. Chuck can examine the action from an objective distance and reflect on what has occurred.

I say to Chuck, "Replay in your mind what the three have said. Close your eyes to see and hear what has been said." I wait. "Now, Chuck, I want you to reach inside and find your own wisdom. Look at them, and with the wisdom you possess, tell them what needs to be done. Remember, you are there in the mirror also."

Chuck says, "The three of you need to let go of the past and try to start over. Mom, in a way I'm like you. You need to stand up for yourself. Dad, you need to see beyond your nose. Chuck, you need to forgive a little bit. You are hanging on to your resentment like it is a security blanket. You also need to be more assertive."

We stand in silence for a moment. I tell Chuck, "For today, I am going to have this scene dissolve. Will you please put those chairs away?" He does.

"What have you learned, and what are you going to do till we meet again?" (*Sharing phase.*)

He answers, "I think I have learned a little about Dad and Mom. They didn't plan things to be this way. I need to try feeling less sorry for myself. Maybe Dad and I could get to know each other better. I think beneath it all, he cares about me. But most important, I think I am a wimp. I need to stand up for myself. I think there really is a more assertive Chuck like the one on the high chair."

We set up another appointment, and Chuck leaves. I note that Chuck needs more practice dialoguing with his father and mother. He also needs another opportunity to do an intrapsychic encounter to examine his own feelings. Finally, I note, "A family conference may be needed after the third or fourth session."

At the next session I ask, "What important things have you been thinking about since we last met?" (*Warm-up.*)

Chuck answers, "Mostly I have been feeling disgusted with me and my family. I don't know why I have such hopeless feelings. Maybe I want them to feel sorry for me."

I want to know if Chuck has any optimism. I ask, "On a scale of 1 to 10, how optimistic are you that you can change?"

He says, "For some reason I feel a little optimistic. I'd say about 4 on a scale of 10."

"Where were you when you first came for help?"

"I guess about 1!"

I ask, "Chuck, do you recall how you arranged the chairs representing hope and despair?"

"Yes."

"Rearrange them showing the way you view their placement today. Remember, the complete you is on the chair by the far wall." He places the "I hate myself" chair slightly beyond the middle of the room and the "I won't give up" chair near the middle of the room.

I ask Chuck to explain what he sees. This is another way to mirror his internal picture.

Chuck answers, "Today I have more hope that things can get better, and I feel less negative about myself. I don't feel as angry as before, but I am afraid that my depression is still just around the corner."

I ask, "What are you going to do to help yourself?"

"I think I need to give myself more credit for what I do and stop blaming everyone else for what goes on in my life. But, that is difficult for me."

I ask, "What do you need to tell your parents so you can become your own person and move on as an adult separate from them?"

"I need to tell them I am almost eighteen years old and that I must make a life for myself. I may never meet their expectations, but I need to stop obsessing about that."

"Do you need to dramatize that?"

"No, I would rather have a session with all three of us here. I may need your help."

When we schedule the family counseling session, Eric will be included. We will use role reversal to teach empathy and understanding.

I am pleased with how far Chuck has come. The important outcome is that he has found the courage to discuss his personal struggles with his parents.

This case shows the process of an *intrapsychic and an interpsychic drama*. It also shows the value of *mirroring and doubling*. Also seen is how quickly the client finds a new way of perceiving the dilemma. Chuck needs to disengage from his persistent addiction to unhappiness before he can perceive his own strength of will. Perhaps several family counseling sessions will help him discover his autonomy. Finally, I am impressed with his intelligence. Most clients do not gather insights as quickly as Chuck. It is obvious that sessions typically have much more detail but for the purpose of teaching this process the session has been compressed.

CHAPTER EIGHT

HANGING ON
AND LETTING GO

This case is about the universal process of disengaging all of us have experienced. Barbara Kantrowitz and Peg Tyre (2006) highlighted the struggle that baby boomer parents face trying to stand aside as their children become independent adults. I use *role reversal* in several ways to help a set of parents disengage from their children.

Sam and Joyce are among the over seventy-six million baby boomers born between 1945 and 1964. These baby boomers are parents to more than eighty million children who enjoy the benefits of the wealthiest and best-educated generation of parents in history, determined to give their children the best possible opportunities. The baby boomer parents have a powerful connection to their children who view them as their best friends. Kantrowitz and Tyre in their May 22, 2006, *Newsweek* article, observe that the close relationship can be a double-edged sword. A comfortable accepting relationship fosters mutual respect, but boomer parents often succumb to fixing problems that rob their children of valuable opportunities to build a sense of self-sufficiency.

Numerous books and other publications offer extensive advice about hanging on and letting go. I published an article about hanging on and letting go in the March 2007 issue of *Counseling Today*. I point out that parents successfully disengage from their children by ushering them through three stages.

The first stage is called *nurturing and protecting* and covers approximately the first ten years of the child's life. These are critical years that lay the foundation upon which children stand for the rest of their lives. During these years, a child discovers that love needs to be unconditional; that boundaries create trust leading

---

to a high self-esteem; and that rules are important to coexist in society. The first stage is the launching pad for the next stage that emerges when the child is about eleven or twelve years old.

The second stage is called *guiding and providing*. Children become introspective and insightful. This stage continues through the end of high school or until the offspring leaves home. Personal identity is formed, and peers become equally or more influential than parents. The resolve of parents to maintain the rules and boundaries is tested to the limits of parental endurance. Nevertheless, during this stage, parents must continue to guide and enforce rules of the family while at the same time expand the boundaries. Mishandling this stage adds to a child's insecurity.

Children cross the threshold to adulthood when they are seventeen or eighteen years old, complete high school, and in some symbolic way, begin their journey toward independence. This is the stage of *meeting and conferring*. Parental love and concern continue into the offspring's adult years, but the mission of molding the child's life is accomplished. *Parents can be there to observe how the young adult lives but should not be there in his or her life.* Many parents say the transition feels abrupt because they have been nurturing, guiding, and providing for at least eighteen years, and they are not ready to step back and watch their children sink or swim. A child's independence, confidence, and self-direction rest on the willingness of parents to disengage and perform the important role to meet and confer.

Boomer parents seem to be comfortable hovering, and their children are comfortable with the attention (Kantrowitz and Tyre 2006). Letting go requires a conscious and deliberate act by everyone involved. Sam and Joyce are both baby boomers and parents of Becky, a college sophomore, and Alice, a high school senior. Sam is an executive with a local bank, and Joyce is a bookkeeper for a local credit union. They both have maintained a close relationship with the two girls who view Sam and Joyce as their best friends.

Sam and Joyce have made child rearing a major focus of their marriage. They shared the triumphs and defeats with the girls through school projects, Girl Scouts, dance lessons, swim clubs, and school athletics. They have always been there for the girls. Now Alice is about to graduate from high school, and both girls will be out of the nest.

Sam and Joyce are feeling apprehensive. Becky is away at college, but they still have Alice on whom to focus their energy. But Alice is about to leave, and they wonder if they have prepared the girls to be independent. They also wonder if they can resume a fulfilling spousal relationship without the girls as an obvious bond. I am reminded of a couple with whom I consulted more than thirty-five years ago. I remember sitting in their living room and immediately was struck by the fact he called her "Mother" and she called him "Dad." They had gradually defined their roles as "Mother" and "Dad" after years of parenting their five boys.

Sam and Joyce know that protecting the girls from demands and burdens of life is not possible. Nevertheless, it is difficult for them to know where to draw the line between indulgence and neglect. They vacillate when the issue comes up. Joyce seems to be especially concerned. She is drawn toward involvement in the girls' day-to-day lives and reducing the burden of school by helping them in any way possible. Sam is concerned that Joyce is treating the girls as if they were both in high school. As a way to make his point, he tells Joyce, "I hardly ever called my parents when I went to college, and I turned out fine."

Joyce responds, "Sam, your parents missed most of your high school football games! We have always been there. I don't want to abandon them when they may need us the most."

Sam is also concerned that the excessive concern about the girls is affecting their marriage. He suggests to Joyce they talk about their disagreements with a neutral party. Since he met me at a local Kiwanis Club meeting, he suggests they come to me for help. Joyce agrees. She is comfortable with the idea because she saw a counselor for a mild anxiety disorder when she left home for college years ago.

I agree to work with them since my relationship with Sam is limited to a casual greeting at Kiwanis meetings. I meet them at my office late on Tuesday. Sam is forty-five years old, and Joyce is forty-six. Becky is nineteen, and Alice is eighteen. I tell them to explain the issue or issues they want to talk about (*warm-up*).

Sam says, "Both our girls, Becky and Alice, will be off to college next year, leaving us with an empty nest. We don't agree on how involved we should be in their lives. We give them our time and make sure they have all the advantages we can afford. Frankly, it is difficult to think of them as being adults on their own, but we know leaving home and letting go is the normal course of life."

Joyce adds, "Sam and I don't agree on this. I think it is all right to stay close. I know other parents who stay in touch every day by phone or e-mail, and I don't see how it interferes with their children. I think Sam is trying to impose his own experiences onto the girls and me."

I ask, "Do you know what your girls think about this?"

Joyce says, "Neither of them thinks it is wrong to talk each day. They have always confided in us, so I don't see why, all of a sudden, we shut them out."

I tell them, "When your girls lived at home, they had your protection and guidance. Now they are young independent adults. You are providing financial support which reinforces the bond. However, boundaries need renegotiating that respects your liberated adult children. We will examine your family system because it has moved to a new stage. The four of you need to be present. I prefer to meet at your house at our next meeting when Becky is home."

Sam says, "The four of us will be available on Friday of next week. Becky will be home, and I think she and Alice will be able to meet with us. We will make sure and confirm that works for you."

I say I can meet and will wait for a call. The next day Sam calls to say all four of them are available on Friday next at their house at 4:00 PM. We meet in their living room. I habitually do family counseling on the family turf. That is where their life unfolds, and that is where they should examine their life together. Everyone seems relaxed and anxious to talk about the matter of leaving home. They tell me they have talked and understand I am there to help them talk things over.

I say to Becky and Alice, "I have shared with your parents that this family has evolved to a new interdependent stage. Throughout your lives, your parents have given you the benefit of their wisdom, created rules, and given you guidance. You are young adults with wisdom of your own, ready to accept the positive and negative consequences of your choices. In short, it is time to reduce psychological dependence on your parents. You now are all adults. As adults, you meet and confer with each other similar to the way you confer with any other adult. This needs to be understood by all four of you. That is why I am here."

I want to find out how accurately they see the issue through each other's eyes in the family system. *Role reversal* is an efficient process. I ask, "I want each of you to stand up and move to the chair just vacated by the person to your left. After you sit down, become that person. Find that person's thoughts and say what that person says. For example, Sam, you are Joyce; Joyce, you are Becky; Becky, you are Alice; and Alice, you are Sam. I want each of you to speak as the other person about this new stage of *meeting and conferring*."

I look at Sam (in the role of Joyce) and say, "Joyce, we will begin with you."

Sam (as Joyce) says, "I think the new stage sucks. I do not want to be left in the dark about what they do. I want to stay in touch! They can tell me when they don't like what I do."

I say, "Becky, you're next."

Joyce (as Becky) says, "I have had the most time away from home. I guess it has not been so bad. Mom seems to be most interested in what I am doing. [Pause] There are times when I give her advice on—," I interrupt.

"Joyce, you are Becky. You began being Joyce with that sentence. Try to be Becky. Say what is in her mind."

Joyce resumes in role as Becky. "Mom often tells me what to do. She only wants to help. But sometimes she tells me what to do, and I feel like she is treating me like a child." (I am surprised that Joyce came up with that.)

"Alice, it is your turn to say how meeting and conferring changes your life."

Becky (as Alice) says, "I think it takes pressure off of me. I worry that Mom and Dad don't approve of the things I do. If they can see me as an adult doing the best I can, I won't second-guess myself so often."

I say, "Sam, it is your turn."

Alice (as Sam) says, "I sort of stay out of most things. I mean I keep up and am interested in what everyone is doing, but I usually get involved when I must or am mad about something. I think I like the idea of everyone thinking like adults."

"Now that everyone has tried to see through the eyes of one other person, that person can challenge or change what was said."

Alice says, "I think Becky was right on. I do worry too much about approval from Mom and Dad."

Joyce says, "I think Sam oversimplified what I feel. I live for my girls. I don't want them to face more pain than necessary. Life is full of disappointments. Why not save them from some of that?"

Becky jumps in with, "Mom, we know you care for us and love us, but too often you want to solve our problems. I sometimes tell you what one of my professor wants in an assignment, but you jump in and tell me almost word for word what I should say to him the next time we meet. That's not what I want. All I want is to share what is going on. I'm not asking for advice. I'm sorry. I know you just want to help."

There is silence. Sam is staring at the carpet. Joyce has tears in her eyes and is looking down at her hands. Becky and Alice are looking at each other with a concerned expression. I have a hunch they are afraid they may have said too much.

I ask, "What is the silence saying to all of you?" (That question is defensible in a variety of methods of counseling. In this case, I am giving "silence" a role they can address.)

Sam says, "Well, I think it says we are hanging on to the stage before this one. What did you call it?"

"Guiding and providing."

"Yea, that's it. That's what we do as parents. We take care of our kids."

"How long do you want to do that?" I ask.

Joyce looks up and says, "I think I am the one who is having the most difficult time letting go. To be honest, my own mother is still trying to tell me what to do rather than just hearing me out, and that still upsets me. I really don't want to be like that. I hear Becky."

"So how do you all want things to change?"

This time Joyce speaks up first. She says, "Let me throw this out. I need to stay in touch with both girls. That is just the way I am. But I will keep in mind they are intelligent adults capable of solving their own problems and making decisions—right or wrong. I will stop being 'my mother.'" She looks at Sam, "What about you, Sam? What do you think?"

Sam responds, "That makes sense to me. I am too much the other way. I need to show more interest."

Becky says, "One of the things I should do more often is show an interest in what you guys are doing. I get caught up in my life and forget to think about what you guys are doing. Maybe I can do better if I think of myself as an adult. I mean, I know I am an adult, but I think I regress when I am around the two of you."

Alice says, "I haven't thought about leaving home until this year. We have always been a close family, sharing most of what goes on. I wonder a lot about being on my own. I have not thought about being an adult the way it is described here today. It scares me a little, but sooner or later, my life falls on my shoulders. If Mom and Dad can let us sink or swim on our own, I know Becky and I are ready."

"I need help, Sam," says Joyce.

"I think we both need to adjust to the empty nest. When either of us hovers too much, we need to talk it over, and I think we need to focus on other things in our lives. I don't mean we want to ignore you two girls. I mean we need to fill the nest with other things," says Sam.

I say, "Guiding and providing takes on a new meaning for all of you. Is it fair to say that all of you are ready to move on to the stage of meeting and conferring?"

They nod their heads in agreement.

I say, "The commitment to move on in no way solves all the problems and issues that exist or will exist. We simply have reframed the idea of disengaging from the past. We have created a new way to organize the journey. I want the four of you to try some *role training*." We are still in the living room. I get my small rope and lay it down so the room is divided in half.

I tell them, "This half of the room is where you are today. Across the rope in the other half of the room is where you are one year from now. We are time travelers. Move across to the future." They step across the rope and are in the other half of the living room.

I say, "Stay in your own role, and show me what it is like twelve months from now when you are home together talking about your lives. You girls are in college, and Sam and Joyce have gone on with their lives. But you have reinvented yourselves. You all have comfortably moved to the "meet and confer" stage. You are comfortable sharing and learning from each other. Do you understand? You are a year older and wiser."

They sit for a moment in silence, gathering their thoughts. Then, Sam begins, "I am glad you girls are able to be home together. What interesting things have been going on in your lives?" I was a little surprised that Sam started. I was expecting Joyce to start.

Becky picks up the created conversation, "Well, I think the most exciting thing that has happened for me is meeting a really nice guy. We aren't serious, but he is very kind and considerate. And bright too."

Joyce jumps in, "This is the first you have mentioned him. Are you happy? What is he like?"

Becky says, "Alice has met him and thinks he is 'grounded.' You'll have to ask her what that means."

Alice says, "He seems adjusted. So many I meet are self-centered, but this one is truly interested in Becky. I'm keeping up with school and don't yet have time for many dates."

Sam says, "You know, thinking of each other on an equal basis is better. It takes away a lot of worrying of how to fix things. But you girls need to always keep in mind that home is still a harbor in any storm."

Joyce says, "Boy, is he getting poetic! But he is right. I feel a little more freedom. I let things go because I trust that you girls can solve your problems."

At this point, I ask, "How is this different than the way things were a year ago?"

Joyce says, "The main thing I feel in the new role is relief. I never thought I would say that, but I think that I took on too much responsibility. I needed to let that go."

They talk about that concept a little longer till I stop them, remove the rope, and let them come back to the present.

Sam, Joyce, and I meet about three more times to reinforce new and more effective ways of communicating. Joyce continues to talk to the girls about two to three times a week, but more important, she restrains the urge to outline solutions to their dilemmas. The girls attend the same college, and Sam has assumed a more personal interest in the girls. They, in turn, have forced themselves to always ask how things are going at home.

I chose this case study because the family is an intelligent and functional family with respect for each other. Not all of the families working through this phase of maturity evolve as smoothly. Those families require much more structure from me; more time working with the parents separate from the children; and with the children separate from the parents. At times, the parental need to control requires therapy to explore where the need is anchored. I have discovered psychodrama to be brief and effective for a full range of issues families bring to the session.

Noticeable was the very limited use of psychodramatic methods. The two techniques were taking on the role of one other person in the family and some brief role training using future projection. Some of the session is in a very traditional talk therapy mode. A mixture is not unusual.

CHAPTER NINE

DEPENDENCY

This case study focuses on a young man who lives with an overprotective and indulgent mother. She protects and guides him as if he were incapable of handling the affairs of his own life. *Role reversal*, *doubling*, and *concretizing abstract emotions* will be used in this case.

Considerable research suggests parental overindulgence has a negative influence on child development. For example, an overprotective mother robs a child of the satisfaction of solving his or her own dilemma, resulting in self-depreciation and feelings of impotency. In turn, these feelings breed unhealthy dependency and anger that breeds narcissism (Ramsey et al. 1996). Grant's mother is controlling and overprotective. She prides herself in providing the comforts of home and advice and passionately assumes responsibility for Grant. Grant has learned to depend on her for most of his needs. They exchange few words, but subdued tension and anger lie below the surface. Their relationship seems symbiotic and has the unhealthy traits of codependency.

Grant's family physician refers him to me with a note that simply says, "I see Grant periodically for an upper gastrointestinal disorder. He seems clinically depressed and agitated."

Grant is twenty-five years old and has been unable to hold a steady job. He works in the construction trades but often is late or absent from work and subsequently loses his job. When he runs out of money, he returns to live with his mother but always tells her it will be temporary.

A counseling objective is to penetrate the passive aggression and pierce the protected pool of anger that surfaces when he feels impotent. Grant comes for the first session, retreating under the shade of his baseball cap. He defiantly slouches into a chair. I need to mollify the situation so Grant feels less oppositional (*warm-up phase*).

"You are uncomfortable being here," I say. (Obviously that is a "client-centered" empathetic statement intended to connect with his discomfort in the moment.)

"I don't see much to be gained by it."

"I would like to get acquainted with you, and we will see where this goes."

He looks at me for a moment, apparently trying to size me up. He then says, "Well, my name is Grant. I live with my mother right now, and I am between jobs. I suppose the doctor sent me here because he thinks I have an attitude or something."

I ask, "What does the word *attitude* mean to you?"

"I suppose it means I don't agree with everything people say."

"And when you don't agree you ...?"

"I get angry."

"It is annoying when people try to tell you what to do," I say. Again, I choose a reflective client-centered statement, hoping to show I am listening and that I want to avoid telling him how to think. But I don't want to annoy him by repeating his phrase.

"I do not like to be treated like I have half a brain."

I want to anchor the session by finding a time when he has recently felt discounted. So I ask, "When was the last time you felt that you have half a brain?"

"With old Stapleton."

"Stapleton is ...?"

"My boss. Or at least he was my boss. I told him I got caught in traffic, but he wouldn't listen."

I ask, "What did you do?"

"I just walked off the job. I know he was under the gun to get that house finished, so I fixed him."

"So you didn't argue with him. You just walked away."

"You bet! He got the message."

"And what message was that?" I asked.

"That nobody screws with me!"

"There are a lot of Stapletons in your life." (I want to open him up a little more, so I presume this was not the first time he felt pushed around.)

"Yes! There is always someone ready to tell me how to live my life. I suppose *you* are getting paid to tell me how I should live my life, right?"

I answered, "I have all I can handle just running my own life. What I am getting paid to do is help you think about your life. How long has the feeling of being controlled by other people been around?"

"I didn't say other people controlled me."

"I misunderstood. What are you telling me?" (I am in no contest with Grant. I need to understand his reality.)

"I am saying that people tell me what to do because they don't think I can do things right." I would like to drill to the core of his anger, but I also know that Grant does not yet trust me with his secrets. The main secret, I hypothesize, is that his mother has psychologically emasculated him.

I deliberately use my erase board because for now Grant is more comfortable sharing on a cognitive level than on a feeling level. The erase board keeps his focus on something external to both of us.

I say, "List the people who have discounted you for one reason or another."

"Oh, that is easy. For one, there is old man Stapleton. Then there are Sanders and most of the other guys I worked for. Let's see, can I list family members?"

"I think we should write down anyone that comes to your mind."

"Mom."

He and I look at the names on the board. I take my time. I want him to think. Then I ask him to rank the people from least to most influential in his life. This is a little devious, but I need to prod him toward his family of origin if I am going to help him.

As expected, he ranks Mom as the most influential in his life. This does not mean that he has opened the door to me. It merely means he trusts me enough to name her.

We talk a few more minutes about what kind of jobs he has held and what he seemed to like the most. I answer questions he has about counseling. For example, he asked if everything is confidential. I give him the standard answer that everything is between us unless I think he may be a danger to himself or someone else.

He says he understood that but asks, "Am I going to need to spill my guts to you?"

I answer, "You are in control of what you say to me. I will help you discover the important things to discuss. There will be times when I will encourage you to put your thoughts into action. I will be there to help every step of the way."

He says, "I'll do what I can, but don't be surprised if I tell you to go to hell."

"I won't."

I look at the clock and tell Grant that our time is up. I thank him for being honest with me and that I want to learn more. We set a time to meet next week. I suggest that he think of other important ideas that may help me understand him better, and I suggest that he write them down for the next meeting.

I want to regulate our relationship, so I decide to set and maintain firm boundaries with Grant. I establish time limits of our sessions and take a no-nonsense attitude during our therapy. It seems that he feels impotent but compensates with an air of indifference. He leaves with his cap pulled down again, so I see only the lower half of his face. I will avoid a contest of wills with Grant.

He walks in for the next session with a somewhat different demeanor. His eyes are still diverted under his cap. His hands rest in his lap while his thin shoulders slump forward.

I ask, "Did you write anything that you can share with me?"

"Yea, but I didn't know what you wanted to know about me."

"I am most interested in knowing what life is like for you."

"I live at home, but I am looking for a job. I don't want to live at home."

"Why?"

"I feel like a kid who has to ask for everything. I am sick of that."

I ask, "What was it like being a kid?" (I take a chance because his attitude about self began there.)

"I suppose the same as with most kids."

I accept the answer because for all I know, that may be the way he sees it. I ask, "Can you tell me more?"

"I guess I was usually quiet. I don't know."

"If you *did* know, what would you say?"

"I'd have to say it was a little crappy growing up."

"In what way?"

"Mom always jumped on me and told me what to do. She still finishes sentences for me. I don't know—she always has advice for me."

I ask, "Do you tell her how you feel about that?"

"I want to, but it comes back to haunt me. She remembers every word I ever say. It is not worth saying anything."

I say, "Last time toward the end of our session, I said there will be times we will put thoughts into action?"

"Yes."

"You said you don't talk much to your mom because she remembers everything and reminds you about it later. I want you to experience what it is like to say whatever you wish knowing it will not come back to haunt you. I want you to bring two of those folding chairs over here in this open space. Open them facing each other. One chair is you, and the other is your mother."

"All right, but I don't see what it will help."

"I do not know if it will help, but let's give it a try. You sit in that chair." We are close to stepping across the frame and into the picture of his life. We will bring his mother into our time and space.

I say, "You are Grant's mom. What is your name?"

"Grace."

"Grace, your son, Grant, and I are talking about his life. Tell me about Grant."

He stays in the role of his mother and responds, "Grant has trouble holding a job. He has trouble following orders. I always tell him what to do, but he never listens. He is getting hard to handle."

I ask Grant to reverse roles. Mother is firmly established in the other chair, so I ask Grant to look at her and tell her that he needs to run his own life. My directness may sound presumptive and controlling, but here is a young man who has passively fought back with passive aggression. I want him to experiment with healthy assertiveness.

Without much passion and still safe under the bill of his cap, he says, "Mother, I want to run my own life."

I say, "Grant, be more assertive!"

Raising his head slightly so his eyes are clearly visible under the cap, he says with more force, "I can run my own life! I don't need you always looking over my shoulder!"

"Tell her what you feel when that happens."

Grant hesitates and says to me, "I don't know about that! I keep my feelings to myself. That is the safe thing to do with her!"

"Grant, give yourself permission to reveal your feelings to her. In the first place, she is not physically here. Secondly, you have the strength and power to express your feelings." I arrange the chairs so the "Mother" chair is facing the "Grant" chair.

I want to create a way for Grant to access his personal power. I set a stool behind him. I tell Grant to turn and look at the stool and see the Grant who has the strength and courage to say things that Grant here today is unable to say.

I say assertively, "Look at the stool. See a different, more assertive Grant on that stool. Can you see him?"

He says yes.

I ask, "Can you see your mother?"

He says, "Yes, she is there, but she seems pissed."

I say, "I want you to go to the stool and be the courageous Grant. He is exactly like you, but he is your *double* with the courage to talk about feelings and any other thing he wants."

Grant sits on the stool. I tell him, "Grant, close your eyes, and see yourself talking to your mother. Now feel the strength to express your feelings because you know there will be no criticism from your mom. Now tell her about the feelings you remember and the feelings you have now."

Grant looks down from the stool and over the chair in front of him to his mother and says, "I feel like a little kid that needs his mommy every time he turns around! You never ask me a question that isn't followed with a bunch of 'you should have done this or that.' Damn, I get tired of that! You never just listen. You always have some damned solution! And you wonder why I don't talk to you anymore—duh!"

I ask him to reverse roles with his mother. In the role of mother, he says, "You are so ungrateful. I have given my life to you. All I have ever asked in return is a little respect. But no—not you. You think the world revolves around you. I have a clue for you—it doesn't!"

He reverses roles (still from the stool) and says, "Mom, you never wanted me to grow up. You want me to stay under your thumb so you can control me. I don't know what went on between you and Dad, and I don't want to know. I have a pretty good idea why he left though! I have the same feeling—I've got to get you off my back. I have to grow up. I can't go on living around you."

Grant wants to disengage and stop stumbling along an aimless journey toward independence. Grant said he wants to get her off his back. In the office, I keep a backpack containing a few small sandbags. The weights are a metaphor of the feelings he expressed about his mother. The weight will *concretize* the abstract feelings. Grant puts both arms through the straps and hoists the pack onto his back.

I say, "You told your mom that you need to get her off your back. Well, the weights you feel on your back represent your mom's ideas for your life. Walk in this circle. Start by deciding if you want your mom off your back. If you want her off your back, tell her why. Slowly walk with her on your back, and tell her what you want to do with this weight. You have the choice to carry the weight or to remove it. Listen to me again. You have a choice—leave things as they are, or change things."

I continue as he walks, "Feel the weight on your shoulders. Feel the weight down your back. What is the weight? What is the weight, Grant?" (In the beginning I walk beside him and quietly urge him to talk. Later I move to the side.)

"It is my duty to her. Yes! That is it! It is my duty."

I interrupt and remind him to talk to her, not to me.

"I always feel I must make you happy since the old man ran off. It is up to me to fix things. But you never let me grow up. You always want me to need you. You don't want to be alone. Well, damn it, I don't give a f—if you are alone. I have a life. I don't want to hurt you, but you have to let go. You have to get off my back."

"Grant, do you *need* her on your back? *Are you hanging on, or is she hanging on?*"

He answers, "No, I don't need her. I can get along without her hanging on."

"It does not sound that she will choose on her own to get off your back. Talk to her!"

"I can't wait for you to do it. It is up to me, but it is so hard!"

I say, "I know it is the hardest thing you must do. Grant, weigh this carefully. Keep in mind that you may choose to carry the weight rather than change things. Many people choose to do that. Other people choose to change the future and let go of the weight. You may choose either direction. You alone can make the decision." I am deliberately using the term *choose* so he understands the ownership of his action.

He keeps walking in the circle, trying to make up his mind. The weight has become part of him. If he lets go, he faces other decisions. He takes his time. I do not rush him. His facial expression is grim. He is conflicted. He keeps walking. I still do not rush him because this must be a decision, not a make-believe exercise.

He stops and begins to remove the backpack. I stop him and say, "Grant, are you sure? You *can* go on this way the rest of your life. Many people do because it is safe and predictable."

He says, "I am sure. I need to get on with it. I need a life." He removes the backpack gently. He carries it to the chair that is the "Mother" chair. He places it in the chair and says, "I know you mean well. But you have never let me grow up. I need to find out if I can do it on my own."

I put the pack and chair away. We just sit and look at each other. I want the power of what he has done to sink in.

Finally, Grant says, "I feel lighter."

"What do you need to do now?"

"I need to move out. She needs to know I am an adult." He stands up and takes off his cap. He extends his hand and says, "I don't know what you did, but I feel better."

"It doesn't matter what I did. But I want you to come back in two weeks to tell me about your successes and failures. Okay?"

"Okay."

Grant comes back in two weeks to tell me that he has a small apartment and is working for McDonald's. He wants to become a manager someday and move to the city. I wish him well. (*Sharing phase.*)

This chapter focuses on the struggle for independence and the insidious trap of dependency. Erikson, in his psychosocial crisis theory of human development, helps understand the journey we travel toward maturity. He suggests movement through the stages is sequential but that we can revisit previous stages to acquire skills missed the first time around. Grant is struggling to successfully pass through Erikson's stage of identity and role confusion, exhibiting difficulty seeing clearly who he is and how to relate positively to his environment (Erikson 1950). At the same time, he is fighting for autonomy, independence, and the ability to think for himself.

To successfully accomplish tasks associated with later stages, we must successfully finish expectations from earlier stages. For example, we overcome our sense of doubt before we can become autonomous. Grant has served his sentence of dependency and is ready to face the world independent of the shackles of self-serving parental demands. Clients often are ambivalent when it comes to freeing themselves from the clutches of such unrelenting hands. This chapter shows how "concretizing" the "weight on my back" becomes a powerful cathartic tool.

Follow-up sessions with Grant suggest that he is finding the strength to be independent, or, perhaps, his independence is giving him strength. He is becoming less narcissistic and more empathetic with those around him. I think he has a reasonable chance to experience a life containing risks and to experience life absent of the fear of surrendering his autonomy.

CHAPTER TEN

FAMILY COUNSELING

This case demonstrates the use of psychodrama in family counseling. A teenage daughter challenges the authority of her parents who are concerned they have lost control. *Role reversal* and *the role of a wisdom figure* are effectively used.

Alonzo and Juanita Martinez are referred by their family physician for help with their fourteen-year-old daughter, Angelica. Angie is belligerent and uncooperative. She complains about helping with household chores and ignores curfews. Her grades have dropped since last year at this time, and her parents are concerned the group with whom she associates is making things worse. Angie is competing with her parents for power and control.

If Angie wins the power struggle with her parents, she will destroy the tree that gives her shade. She will demolish the shelter that can shield her during these tumultuous years. Alonzo and Juanita have become ensnared by the regressive narcissistic antics of this immature adolescent girl (Dreikurs 1968).

None of this convicts Angie as a monster resolute on disengaging from her parents. She is a self-absorbed adolescent. She wants independence but needs nurturing and firm boundaries. She needs guidance and direction from parents willing to set limits and endure the challenges.

About forty years ago, Stanley Coopersmith (1967) wrote an insightful book, *Antecedents of Self-Esteem.* Coopersmith asserted that firm boundaries make happy children. His research showed that firm, consistent, and caring behavioral limits are the antecedents of well-grounded and secure adults. His conclusions are as applicable today as when they were written.

In short, Alonzo and Juanita are losing ground. They are locked with Angie in a power struggle that frequently escalates into a shouting match and Angie storming to her room. Alonzo and Juanita are fearful that Angie will run away from home. I make an appointment to see the family in their home. As I have stated, I usually work with a family in their home because concerns are addressed and solved more easily in the home where the issues arise.

I arrive at the Martinez home on Tuesday. The *warm-up* phase of our encounter is short. We introduce ourselves, and I ask the three to tell me what they hope to accomplish. The parents both say they want to learn how to be better parents, and Angie pouts, saying nothing. I decide they will warm up as we move into action.

I ask, "Where in the house is the family usually together?" They agree it is at the dinner table. We all go to the dining area, and I tell Angie to arrange the family members so I see where each person usually sits. She hesitates briefly, looks around and, finding no objection, shows me. I choose Angie to assist me because I want her cooperation. I empower her to be part of this therapeutic process.

The parents are seated at the opposite ends of the oval oak table. Angie is on the side, with her back to the windows and the backyard. I stand, positioning myself to the left of Alonzo. The dining area is an extension of the kitchen, forming an L shape along the back side of the house. Beyond the dining area is the living room. The surroundings lend a comfortable, homey atmosphere.

I thank Angie for her help and ask, "What do you talk about during dinner?" I wait. Finally, Alonzo says, "The last six months have been quiet. We just don't talk much."

My primary objective today is to teach them the process of *role reversal*. "I want all of you to stand up and move into the chair to your left. When you are in that chair, you will become that person. For example, Angie, when you move to your dad's chair, you will become him and your words will be his. Do not worry if you are right or wrong—that does not matter. What matters is that you become him for that moment." Angie sits in Alonzo's chair. Alonzo becomes Juanita, and Juanita becomes Angie. I need to interview each of them in this new *role*. I want them to *experience* being the other person—*not pretend*. Counseling a family using this three-dimensional approach is a slow and deliberate process—but then, family counseling, regardless of the therapeutic approach, is time-consuming.

I move around to the long side of the table next to the window, where Juanita now assumes the role of Angie. I put my hand on her shoulder to firmly anchor her in the role and ask, "Angie, what things are important in your life?"

Juanita (as Angie) answers, "My friends."

I move to Angie (in the role of Alonzo), and I ask, "Alonzo, where do you work?"

"I work for the Johnson Manufacturing Co. I am in charge of a department."

I continue, "Alonzo, what is important in your life?"

Angie (as Alonzo) answers, "My work."

"What worries you about Angie?" I ask.

"I am afraid she will get into trouble."

I move to the other end of the table where Alonzo is waiting to respond in the role of Juanita. By now he knows what I expect.

I ask, "Juanita, what is important in your life?"

"To be a good mother."

"Anything else?"

"To be a good wife."

I tell them to return to their original places at the table. "This is your opportunity to modify what has been said. Angie, is there anything you need to change that your mom said?"

Angie says, "She is right—my friends are important. I also care what Mom and Dad think of me, but they're afraid that I am going to embarrass them."

I ask, "Alonzo, was Angie correct? Is your work the most important thing in your life?"

He answers, "Work has to be important, but my family is the most important thing in my life. Why would I take time to do this if it isn't important?"

I ask, "Juanita, was Alonzo correct? Being a good mother and wife are the important things in your life?"

"I guess that pretty much sums it up. I don't have anything else more important."

To this point, each has reversed roles with one other person in the family. I have accomplished my goal—they understand the process. In this case, Angie spoke as her dad; Alonzo spoke as his wife; and Juanita spoke as Angie. If I had rotated counterclockwise, I would have heard different responses and collected different data. My immediate objective is to enable them to focus through the eyes of another person in the family, to *empathize*. *Ultimately, change will depend on empathy.* It is not my goal at this time to collect information. That will come later.

Angie's narcissism has *not* been appropriately challenged. She has been allowed to concentrate on satisfying her personal needs with little concern for the needs of others. She enjoys being at the center of her small universe. Alonzo and Juanita likely have neglected to establish firm and consistent boundaries from the time Angie was a toddler. Narcissistic symptoms are common for an adolescent and do not mean Angie has a narcissistic personality disorder. Nonetheless, if the parents do not maintain consistent boundaries, or are reluctant to exercise adequate discipline, such a personality disorder may evolve.

The three of them are facing a challenge. Angie learned at an early age that she gets attention just as easily by misbehaving as by behaving properly. Unfortunately, she also learned how to control the temperament and the behavior of her parents. Angie is belligerent, which conceals her unconscious cry for the security of rules and boundaries. The crucial question is, *Can the parents change what they are doing?*

We meet in the living room at our next session. I tell them to bring the dining room chairs to the living room because I want to avoid letting them select a comfortable living room chair. I ask them to arrange the chairs in a triangle so two people may not appear to be united against the other.

I begin with my observations. "Mr. and Mrs. Martinez, parenting is a very difficult task. Angie did not come with a set of instructions, but you are doing the very best you can. Your greatest challenge is deciding what Angie's boundaries should be."

"Angie, you are fourteen, but you want to be sixteen or seventeen. You do not want to be told what to do. We are going to find a way for the three of you to live together under this roof." Angie immediately folds her arms and turns in her chair. Alonzo and Juanita look at me with a wide-eyed expression of dread and doubt.

I say, "Juanita, will you and Angie switch roles, please?"

My plan is to let the two of them *experiment with the other's role* and see what they discover. Eventually all of them must discover the world through the eyes of the other. Reconstruction of this family depends on it.

I look at Juanita (in the role of Angie) and say, "Angie, tell your mom and dad how difficult it is to be fourteen."

Juanita (as Angie) says, "I feel like I am sixteen, and it seems I should be able to do all the things a sixteen-year-old should do. I get mad when you don't let me do things I want to do. I am going to sneak around behind your back if you don't let me do what I want."

I turn to Angie who now is in the role of her mom. I ask, "Mom, talk to Angie about this." I am interested in hearing what Angie says as Juanita.

"Angie, you are not sixteen. You are fourteen. I'm not much help to you. I don't know what a fourteen-year-old girl should be like. I was never allowed to be fourteen or even sixteen, for that matter, because I had to take care of my sisters and brothers!"

I tell them to return to their own role. This is new information for me, so I am curious about Juanita taking care of siblings. I also am interested in knowing if there is anger connected to the comment. Is Angie angry that her mother is not giving guidance?

I ask Juanita, "A moment ago when Angie was speaking as you, she said you took care of your siblings and did not get to experience your teen years like other girls. Tell me more about that."

"I was the oldest of ten kids and had to take care of my brothers and sisters. I guess I didn't have much of a life back then. I want Angie to get what I missed. I don't know why she is so unhappy about that!"

I allow some silence for reflection. I notice that Angie no longer has her arms folded across her chest, and there is a somber expression on her face. Juanita is looking at Alonzo who is looking down and twirling his thumbs. It appears that he has no idea what to say.

I ask Angie and Juanita to reverse roles again. I ask Angie (in the role of Juanita), "Mom, tell Angie more about being one of the oldest in a large family."

"Well, there were too many kids for Grandma—sorry—for Mom to take care of, so I had to step in. Because of that, I didn't get to do much else. I felt cheated. So now I want Angie to get what I was cheated out of."

I ask them to return to their own chairs. In her own role, I ask Angie, "Keep in mind what was just said and tell me how you think this is affecting your life." I am shifting out of dramatizing to direct questions and answers from the family members.

Angie tells me, "I like that my mom is my friend. Many of my friends have moms that are a lot stricter. I am sorry she worked so hard when she was my age, but that doesn't mean I need to work that hard. I know both my mom and dad are mad at me because I don't always mind them, but I don't think they understand what it is like to be a kid today."

"Angie, do you think your mother's life affects what she does with you?" I ask.

"I suppose she wants me to have what she didn't get."

I ask, "Alonzo, what do you see going on here?"

"I think Angie has figured out Juanita's hot buttons. The one that works best for Angie is acting hurt and deprived, which really upsets Juanita. That is when Juanita and I argue the most. I know Angie is conning us, but Juanita thinks Angie might lose a friend or two. I really don't care if she does. We are going in three different directions."

I say, "Next week we will look at that. In the meantime, Angie, I want you to watch your friends and decide who shows empathy and who does not. I also want you to decide if you show empathy. Do you know what that means?"

Angie says, "Yes. It is feeling what another person feels."

"That is an excellent answer. You will do well with the assignment."

"Alonzo and Juanita, I want you to spend at least two hours this next week making a list of the privileges and consequences to give Angie. She needs to know exactly where she stands. She needs to know the rewards for choosing to follow the rules, and she needs to know the consequences when she chooses not to follow the rules. I want you to pay special attention to how she can earn credit when she follows the rules."

They both agree. Angie is listening but shows little emotion. It appears that she is a willing participant but will reserve judgment.

We meet in the living room a week later on the dining room chairs. I say, "Angie, last week I asked you to practice your empathy skills. What did you learn?"

"I noticed that a lot of people really don't mean what they say. They pretend to like me, but I can tell they are lying."

"How can you tell that?"

"I don't know. I guess it is the way they look and act."

I say, "Sometimes a person's expression and body language tell us more than anything else. You are very observant."

Alonzo says, "The session last week helped me understand Juanita. I am trying hard to see the world that Angie sees, but I don't know if I am right."

Juanita says, "I have thought about what I missed when I was Angie's age, and I guess I don't want to deprive her. Alonzo and I think I may let Angie talk me into letting her do things that are not good for her."

Angie jumps in with both feet. "I suppose now you and Dad are going to make me stay home and not let me do anything. I was afraid this would happen!" Angie returns to her brooding posture, half turned with her arms folded, and Alonzo and Juanita turn to me with an expression of "now what?"

Knowing that Angie is intentionally challenging the process, I decide to psychodramatically empower her. I say, "Angie, right now I want you to become the *wisdom figure* for this family. The wisdom figure has the responsibility of helping everyone make wise choices. You will listen and help. For example, Angie, when your mom and dad are talking things over, you will listen carefully so that when I ask for advice from the wisdom figure, you will be able to give that advice. Do you understand?"

"I guess, but how will I know what advice to give?"

"It will be advice from the wisdom figure—not from you."

"But I still won't know!"

I said, "When the time comes, you will know. I will be there to help you."

She indifferently responds, "Yeah, okay—whatever!"

I address Alonzo and Juanita and say, "Turn your chairs so that you face each other. Thank you. Your first task relates to *boundaries*. You will talk to each other about the regulations and rules that you think this family should live by. These rules apply to everyone."

"Angie, you stand on that chair so the wisdom figure has a good look down at everyone, and listen to what is said."

I ask Alonzo and Juanita to talk about *universal family rules* because I do not want to put Angie on the defensive yet. The following is a portion of the dialogue between Alonzo and Juanita:

Alonzo says, "Maybe a family rule could be that we pick up after ourselves."

Juanita says, "Yes, and maybe there should be a rule where we say please and thank-you! We should respect one another."

I turn to the wisdom figure and ask, "Wisdom Figure, what do you say about these ideas."

Angie looks at me as if to say, "You've got to be kidding!"

I say, "Go ahead. Tell them if those two things make sense and if this family can follow them."

She looks down on them and says somewhat cynically, "Yes, this family can do that."

I turn back to Alonzo and Juanita and ask, "What else?"

Juanita says, "I think we should eat supper together." Alonzo adds, "Whenever we can, because sometimes our schedules don't fit." Juanita rejoins, "But, maybe we need to plan to eat together every evening and agree on the exceptions."

Since there seems to be a slight disagreement, I ask for advice from the wisdom figure. This will be a test for her. I will find out if Angie can get outside of her self-centered tendency long enough to think of benefits for the group. Family rules are *group norms* initially established by the parents because the generation boundary gives them the authority. I am not giving Angie veto power. I am allowing her to give an opinion.

I turn to Angie (wisdom figure) and ask, "Wisdom Figure, make a helpful suggestion to them. What is best for everyone?" Angie says, "It is important that we eat together as long as we agree to talk to each other. If we do not talk, there is no reason to even consider this rule."

I think to myself, *She probably is right.*

Juanita says, "I agree. We will talk." Alonzo agrees.

Another rule the parents bring up has to do with calling each other when any one of them discovers he or she will be home later than agreed.

Angie stalls on this rule. She looks down from her wisdom position and hesitates. Finally, she says, "Why do we need this rule?"

Alonzo looks up at her and, with a tone of unusual patience, says, "Because in this day and age, we need to know everyone is safe."

I think Angie finds herself lodged between a rock and a hard place. She cannot ignore the wisdom of such a response nor can she argue for complete autonomy, especially while being the wisdom figure. She says, "Everyone will follow this rule. When parents are not home when they say, they will call. When the daughter is not home when she says, she will call." I think she is surprised by what she just said.

There is one very important issue with which they must deal. Alonzo and Juanita need to agree on boundaries for Angie. They are enabling Angie to "divide and conquer" and consequently manipulate the rules. Presently Juanita is afraid to enforce the rules, partly because she lacks appropriate modeling from her own childhood and partly because she is fearful that Angie will be angry with her. Alonzo, on the other hand, tries to compensate by being extra firm with Angie.

Angie is too close to this issue and cannot be the wisdom figure. I tell Angie to step down and sit on the chair. I decide I will consult with Alonzo and

Juanita while Angie observes. I assume a very traditional counseling role sitting on a chair across from them. I ask, "What do you believe Angie's boundaries should be?"

Alonzo says, "I think Angie needs to stay home on school nights and that her curfew on Friday and Saturday nights should be eleven o'clock. As we said a while ago, if she cannot meet her curfew, she will need to call to explain. I also think she needs to help around the house. She should keep her room clean and help Juanita with the housework."

Alonzo seems very definite, so I ask, "Alonzo, your ideas seem to have been thought out carefully. Have you and Juanita talked this over?"

"Yes, we have, but we have not come to an agreement on the punishment if Angie does not follow the rules."

Alonzo and Juanita eventually agree to the rules and also the consequences for Angie when she chooses to ignore the rules. For example, if she is out after curfew the third time, regardless if she calls, she loses the privilege of her cell phone while she is home. I write everything on the erase board, and they transcribe the conclusions to a document that eventually all of them sign.

As you can imagine, Angie is not happy with everything, yet she signs the family agreement. They create a statement that sets down the positive and negative consequences of her choices. She can earn credits and privileges in addition to losing them. I think the idea of earning privileges appeals to Angie.

We meet the following week and decide to do a future-projection exercise. We meet in the living room, but rather than bring chairs to the room, I lay the rope on the floor so it divides the room.

I say to them, "This side of the rope is the present. The other side of the room is five years into the future. As you step across the rope, you are into that future. All of you will be five years into the future. You will be adults. You will have survived the past five years. You will be in the present, but the present will be in the future. You will be free to spontaneously create your reality in the moment five years from now. You are there during the Christmas vacation. I will be back here five years ago.

"As soon as you step over the rope, you will feel yourself five years into the future. You are on your own to talk about what life is like as adults for each of you. When you are ready, step over the rope and into the future."

Hesitantly, they step across the rope and stand in silence looking at each other. Finally, Alonzo looks at Angie and says, "My goodness, you turned out to be a beautiful adult!"

Angie looks at her dad and then, with an astonished look, says, "Thank you, Dad. I was not expecting that. When I was a teenager, I never felt pretty. In fact, I sort of felt ugly most of the time. I think I made life hell for you and Mom. I think things began to change about four or five years ago. We began to feel like a family. A sociology class at college makes sense to me because of what we went through."

Juanita is smiling. "Those four or five years seem so long ago. I wanted so much for you to be happy I almost gave up on myself. But with you and Dad's help, I no longer had to make everyone feel better. You may not believe this, but I grew up—even at that age! And, Angie, you helped."

Alonzo stands there listening and says, "I think I once said that family is the most important thing to me. I think what I like most now is we are all adults. I don't have to worry about raising kids anymore! Come. Let us put our arms around each other and make this the best Christmas ever."

They hug for a moment. I hear a sniffle or two. They turn to me, and I know they are ready to step back over the rope to join me.

I ask, "Did that turn out the way you wanted, or is there more you want to create?" They look at each other and shake their heads. I say, "Step back to my time."

I remove the rope and ask what they discovered.

Surprisingly, Angie speaks first. She says, "Somehow, being out there in the future, the things going on now don't seem so big. Why is that?"

I ask, "Who wants to tackle the answer to that?"

Juanita says, "I think it is because we were able to get far away enough from it to see things in perspective? Is that right? [She looks at me.]"

I say, "I think you captured the answer. Perhaps when things seem to be overwhelming, you can remember this moment when you all looked back from the future!"

I meet with the family three more weeks and then meet once a month for the next three months. We do *role training* to experience different roles they will play in the future. They examine various responses to hypothetical and real situations. These sessions are helpful because the family experiments with the negative and positive roles they anticipate playing during future predicaments.

The family makes the greatest strides when they meet with me as a family. I also meet alone with Angie and also once with Alonzo and Juanita during the time we work on the issues. Looking back on the work with the family, I am convinced that the success was related to the ownership they assumed for their own success. For example, they defined success and failure for themselves, and at times, each assumed the role of wisdom figure.

Angie is beginning to feel she has an important role in the family. Juanita is distinguishing her teen years from Angie's, and Alonzo's demeanor has softened. He is much less autocratic when he considers solutions to family issues.

The case gives an example of how psychodrama can be applied to family therapy. We used *role reversal* and *future projection* and frequently employed the *wisdom figure*. Enjoining their wisdom rather than mine obviously gives them ownership.

CHAPTER ELEVEN

AGING

A young man asks an elderly man, "Have you lived here all your life?" The elderly man replies, "Not yet." Today's aging population is living longer than any previous generation, requiring counselors to understand issues being considered by our aging population. As the nation's seventy-six million baby boomers retire, the total demand for professional counseling increases. By 2030, the number of older Americans will have more than doubled to approximately seventy million. Aspirations and ambitions of the current aging society differ from those of the past generations. For example, older adults remain more physically and emotionally healthy than their cohorts of previous generations. The opportunities lying before them are appealing and seem within reach. They are more concerned than previous generations are about the meaning of life and their legacy. This is the story of Clara. From all outward standards, Clara has lived a successful life, and yet she contemplates how to find fulfillment.

We view the "winter" of our lives through a new window. The view and our questions are new and yet common to almost all people sharing this journey. We want our lives to have meant something worthwhile.

Jung (1934), the analytical psychologist, is credited for saying, "As we age we become more ourselves." For example, if we have been optimistic most of our lives, perhaps we will be even more optimistic in the final years. Then again, I suspect a pessimist becomes even more pessimistic. At any rate, if Jung is correct, our personal characteristics become exaggerated. I cannot speak for anyone else, but that makes me a little nervous at my age.

Back to Clara. I have known Clara for years. We first met twenty-five years ago when she was a fifty-year-old professor of English at the university. Her husband died two years ago, and she has recently celebrated her seventy-fifth birthday. Last week, Clara called to make an appointment for professional counseling. After deciding that my casual acquaintance with Clara will not create a dual relationship, we make an appointment.

This is a brief and relatively simple case report. Clara wants to feel worthwhile during the remainder of her life. Clara is an intelligent and gregarious woman who remains active in the community. I ask Clara how I may help. She tells me that making the transition to retirement was relatively easy, but recently she has been obsessing about the remaining years of her life.

She says, "My feelings about being seventy-five are very confusing to me. On the one hand, I am thankful for my good health and the opportunities to travel and stay active. On the other hand, I have begun to fixate on my remaining years. I think I am afraid that I may spend them carelessly. Lately I wonder how I will be remembered. But that seems a little silly because when I'm dead, it really won't matter to me!" she says with a chuckle.

Clara has a dilemma. She is presently satisfied with her life but is afraid she may squander the remaining years. I use an erase board and draw a vertical line down the center. The left side is headed Satisfactions and the right side is headed Fears.

I say, "Clara, list the satisfactions you feel about your life here on the left, and list your fears here on the right." She takes the dry marker and on the left begins with her satisfactions. She lists *successful teacher*, *healthy*, *friends*, and *financially secure*. On the right side under Fears, she lists *being selfish*, *becoming lonely*, *living too long*, *not being missed after I die*, and *finding nothing to live for*.

When I hear a client express words like, "On the one hand I feel—, but on the other hand I feel—," the best approach is to give a voice to these parts.

I place two folding chairs side by side. I unfold a third chair and set it across from the other two chairs. The third chair represents Clara here with me in the office, aware of the internal struggle between her satisfactions and fears. She needs to create a persona for the different parts. I begin, however, with Clara in the third chair. The third chair is the complete Clara and must be anchored there. I ask, "Look at the two parts you identified. In a moment you will become each part."

I ask Clara to sit in the "Satisfaction" chair and say, "You are the part of Clara that feels quite satisfied with how her life has evolved. Explain to the complete Clara here in this chair beside me how you came to be."

"Well, she—[I stop her and prompt her to use the personal pronoun *I*]" She begins again. Looking at the chair she just vacated, she says, "I exist because you followed your passion in all parts of your life. You decided to become educated. You married someone you loved. You saved for your retirement. You took care of yourself."

I ask, "Are you the part of Clara that has kept her focused?"

"Yes. I am the voice in her head that keeps her eyes on her goals."

I say, "Reverse roles with the complete Clara." She moves over to the chair facing the other two chairs. I continue, "Clara, you heard the part of you satisfied with life. Respond to it. Affirm or correct anything you heard."

Clara says, "You are correct. You are that logical and very determined part of me. The thing you did not mention is how the drive to succeed has sometimes ignored the needs of other people. For example, you didn't say that my drive to become a professor ignored some of the needs of my husband and two children. By listening to you, I sometimes become selfish."

I say, "Now reverse roles with the part of yourself you have identified as 'fears.'"

She moves over to the chair, and I say, "You are the part of Clara that is afraid her life will end before she is finished. Explain that more clearly to the Clara here with me."

"Clara, you have been too focused all of your life. I know, you took time to have a couple of kids, and you had a marriage, but when it gets right down to it, you are neglectful to those you love and perhaps to yourself. You have never taken the time to enjoy the life you have. It has always been one goal after the other, but you have been afraid to enjoy yourself. What memories will you cherish when it comes to the end of your life? Who is going to say, 'Clara was a joy to be with'?"

I ask her to reverse roles. She sits silently for a moment, looking at the empty chair from which she just heard some indictments. I wait a moment and ask her to respond to that part of her.

Clara says, "I think it is important that I hear from you. I still have some important years left, and maybe I need to worry less about everyone else and enjoy me more. The legacy I want to leave is an example of someone who knew how to be happy and live life that God gave me."

I ask, "What can you tell these parts of yourself so they create less stress for you?" Clara says, "Both of you are important for me, but you both need to be moderate. I can feel proud of what I have done, and I also need to relax and be less driven. I am going to listen to both of you but in a new way." (Moreno, founder of psychodrama, would probably recognize this as a slice of spontaneity-creativity and catharsis of integration.)

"Clara, are you taking something new away with you today?"

"Yes. I am okay with me. I need to trust me more. I think I will look at each day as a new adventure. That will help me. Thank you."

I ask her to call me in a month to tell me how she is doing with her life. Clara is facing a very common dilemma. As we age, we transition. The success of our transition depends not only on how well we can objectively let go of patterns of living that have worked well during the bulk of our adult life but also begin to carve out new paths and passions. We can learn to exult in our own presence. Sometimes we need help.

I believe the brevity of this session is related to the action-oriented use of role reversal that is a product of the psychodramatic methods created by the genius of J. L. Moreno. This is a very brief and clear-cut example of the multiple approaches set forth by Moreno. I find clients are productively introspective when they psychodramatically confront themselves. Clients spend less time trying to explain issues to the counselor. The counselor has the luxury of observing the action and learning from the client, while the client hears his or her own dilemma with personal clarity. Clara viewed an old dilemma in a new way and resolved to modify her choices. Her creativity and spontaneity are at the core of psychodrama.

CHAPTER TWELVE

UNRESOLVED GUILT

This chapter involves an encounter with God. A young man does a *role reversal with God* and reframes his picture of the accident in which his life partner died.

It is a dark, quiet night as Trevor and Hal drive home from a concert in a nearby town. They are talking about the concert as Trevor maneuvers the winding road home. Trevor still sees the eyes of the deer reflected in the car's headlights. He hits the brakes and swerves to the left in an effort to avoid hitting the deer. Trevor survives the devastating accident, but Hal, his companion of three years, dies instantly.

Trevor relives those terrifying seconds like an unrelenting nightmare. He is convinced that he should have done something to avoid hitting the deer. It is all so real and yet surreal. One moment they are laughing and enjoying the evening, and the next moment, Trevor's world changes forever.

It has been six months since the accident. Trevor feels suicidal under the weight of his guilt. Through tears and a halting voice, he tells me his story. He sits staring down at his hands tightly folded in his lap.

After a brief silence, I ask, "What do you need?" (*Warm-up.*)

Trevor looks up and says, "I am not sure. I want to feel better—less guilty—but that sounds selfish because I think I should feel guilty. After all, I was the one driving!"

I reflect, "To let go of the guilt somehow diminishes the importance of your relationship with Hal."

Trevor looked up and says, "Yes, I am torn between getting on with my life and the thought of abandoning Hal." Trevor looks back down at his folded hands with his shoulders slumped forward. His body language proclaims despair.

I ask, "Trevor, what do you need to do in order to move on?" There are two reasons for the question. First, I need information so I know where to begin. Second, Trevor needs to know *he is responsible for growth and change.*

Trevor looks at me, and then looks back down at his lap, obviously uneasy. "I know that I need to get on with my life, but I feel so depressed. My depression almost immobilizes me. I do not know how to control it."

I ask, "What do you think Hal would tell you to do?"

"I have no doubt he would tell me to get on with my life."

"Have you forgiven yourself for the accident?"

Trevor looks up again and, after a brief hesitation, says, "No. I guess not. It seems too unforgivable."

I say, "In other words, you are choosing to continue this way."

"No. I don't want to keep on this way, but I feel too guilty for a full pardon."

I prop the erase board on the easel and ask Trevor, "What words define who you are? Imagine words on a sign hanging from your neck."

Trevor thinks for a moment and says, "I am a loser."

I ask, "What else?"

"I am guilty."

I ask, "Is that the complete description of who you are?"

"No, I guess I am a man who cares about other people."

"So, there are many parts to you. Hal loved you as that caring person. Is that right?"

"Yes, that was something we liked in each other."

I say, "You would do about anything to honor Hal, wouldn't you?"

"Yes."

"Could it be that you honor him most by getting on with your life?"

Trevor straightens himself a little and says, "I know you are right, but I don't want to."

I delicately broach the subject of an interaction with Hal. "You and Hal were very close and shared many things when he was alive. Trevor, if we bring the presence of Hal here to this room, will you talk through your feelings with him?"

Trevor answers, "I have talked with Hal in my mind many times. He was there one moment and gone the next! I didn't have a chance to tell him how much he meant to me."

I tell Trevor, "I want to hear the words that are in your head. Please recall those thoughts, walk in a circle, and let me hear your thoughts. It's called a *soliloquy.* Do you understand?"

Trevor answers yes. I am asking this to capture the depth of self-incrimination.

Trevor begins walking. His eyes are almost closed. He says, "Hal, I don't think I can go on without you. You would be alive except for me. I will trade places with you, but I don't know how. I am stuck. I don't know what to do!"

I say to Trevor, "I think you need to deal with *unfinished business*. I want you to sit in the chair across from you and become Hal. I will help you."

Trevor seems to understand, but it is obvious that we are walking into a delicate area. I gently say, "Please sit in that chair and be Hal." (*Action phase*.)

Trevor moves to the empty chair and nervously looks at me. I say, "Hal, I know you and Trevor were very close. Tell me how old you were when you died in the car accident." I begin with a nonintrusive question and do not avoid mentioning Hal's death.

"I was twenty-eight years old, a year younger than Trevor."

I say, "I have met Trevor, but I want to know you." Asking Hal about his life also provides information about Trevor.

Hal answers, "Trevor and I were accountants with the same firm. I met Trevor at work several years ago."

"Tell me more," I say.

"Trevor and I have been partners for over three years. He is the kindest person I know, but he also demands too much of himself. He tries to make everyone happy, sometimes ignoring his own needs. It took him a long time to tell his family about us, but they have accepted us as a couple more easily than he thought they would. Now he has almost cut himself off from everyone. I don't think he knows what to do."

I say to Hal, "Since the accident, Trevor has been depressed and seriously struggling to accept your loss. It happened so quickly neither of you was able to say good-bye. Trevor needs to talk to you about his feelings and deal with the unfinished business. Are you okay with that?"

Hal says, "Yes."

I say, "Reverse roles. Please move to Trevor's chair." He moves to the other chair and sits down.

I continue, "Trevor, we have as much time as you need with Hal. Decide where you want to begin. For example, I know you want to tell him about your feelings of loss."

Trevor turns toward the empty chair, which, for Trevor, it is no longer empty. Hal is there in the chair. His intense focus penetrates the space between the two chairs.

He says, "Hal, I miss you so very much. My life has lost meaning. I do not know what to do." With that, Trevor breaks down and cries. I wait to allow the catharsis to run its course and resist an impulse to console him. Comforting him would respond to my need, not his. In addition, this is a journey he must travel alone.

I give him verbal reassurance. "Trevor, take your time." At the same time, I process what has happened and create scenarios in my mind. For example, I suspect that Trevor's tears are reflecting guilt and pain.

I ask, "Trevor, what are your tears saying?" (I realize this breaks the flow of the action, but I see no need to have Trevor reverse roles with his tears; nevertheless, role reversal with the tears can be helpful as another psychodramatic choice.)

"They are saying I am sorry."

"Tell Hal."

"Hal, I am so sorry. If I would have just turned the car the other way, you would be alive."

I say to Trevor, "Tell Hal what you need."

Trevor looks at Hal and says, "I feel so much guilt. I cannot let go of it. I need your forgiveness—even just a little."

I tell Trevor to reverse roles, and without hesitation or prompting, Hal says, "Trevor, it was an accident. I know that you would have done anything to avoid it. I know that you would take my place. You must believe me when I say I forgive you. I forgive you! Trevor, we had over three years of a wonderful life together. Life sometimes ends like this. We enjoyed each day together. You will need to learn to welcome each new day without me. You need to move on."

The session is about over, and Trevor needs to respond to Hal's comments, and also he needs to end the encounter in his own role, so I ask him to reverse roles. Trevor moves to his own chair, and I tell him to respond to Hal.

"Hal, I know you are right, but I still feel guilty even if it doesn't make sense. I know I need to get on with my life. I'll think about what you have said."

I tell Trevor, "Our time is about up, so we will let Hal go for today. I want to meet with you next week at the same time. Between now and then, please write a one-page letter to Hal explaining what you plan to do with this leftover guilt."

We set up an appointment for next week, and Trevor leaves. I go to my desk and note in his chart that he is warmed up to the process of psychodrama and that guilt is the first manifestation of his struggle. I am thinking that we should begin the next session with a brief warm-up encounter with Hal and continue to look closely at the guilt factor. The unyielding guilt that Trevor feels about the accident keeps him bound to the incident. Trevor needs to embrace his relationship with Hal and simultaneously get on with his life by letting go of the tragedy. Trevor's spiritual compass continues to pull him toward a struggle with guilt and forgiveness. I need to explore this with him.

At the next session, I ask if he wrote the letter to Hal as I suggested. He says yes and gives me a copy. The letter to Hal essentially explains his feelings of regret and responsibility. He tries to tell Hal that it does not seem right to ignore the feelings of guilt. He wrote, "I would feel guilty not feeling guilty!"

I have worked with clients whose spiritual life frequently plays a significant role in their quest to resolve guilt issues. Therefore, I ask, "Are you a spiritual person?"

"Yes. My spiritual life has always been important to me."

I ask, "Do you need to hear from God?"

This question must have taken him by surprise because he looked up with a startled expression. Trevor has confined himself within the cloak of guilt from which escape seems almost impossible. His spiritual convictions may expose a path through his guilt. I tell Trevor he needs to reverse roles with God.

He says, "Isn't that a little presumptive? I cannot be God!"

"Perhaps not, but *if you could be God*, let's find out what he says." Such a hypothetical statement frees the client to wonder. I place one chair facing a tall stool. I want God to be elevated a few inches above Trevor, so I use a stool because I do not have elevated floors in my office. I ask Trevor to sit in the lower chair and look up to the stool. To ensure that he is grounded in his own role, I ask, "Do you know why you are here, Trevor?"

"I am going to talk to God about my feelings."

I ask Trevor, "Where is a place that gives you a sense of God's presence?" I find it important to set a scene for an encounter with God. I think God takes on greater omnipotence.

"Alone on the prairie where I grew up. It is spring, and the grass is rolling in the wind like the sea. It is quiet, and I feel God's presence."

"Will you take me there?"

Trevor responds yes and says, "I am sitting on a hill, it is spring, and the prairie grass is green and tall. The gentle breeze is making the grass appear to be rolling waves. I can smell the fresh air and hear the meadowlarks signaling to each other. It is so peaceful."

"Do you feel God present?"

"Yes."

I point to the stool and tell Trevor, "Please reverse roles with God." Trevor moves from his chair to the stool where he looks down at the empty chair from a slightly higher angle.

I say, "What is your name?"

"I am God."

"What does Trevor believe about you?"

After a slight hesitation, Trevor, in the role of God, says, "He believes I am all-powerful, but I am like a loving father. He prays to me and believes that I can answer his prayers."

I make eye contact with Trevor in the role of God and say, "Trevor's heart is heavy with guilt, and he needs to talk to you about it." I essentially establish the direction of Trevor's dialogue with God. Focusing the action and maintaining control is an essential role of the counselor/director.

I immediately direct Trevor to reverse roles.

Trevor looks up at the stool where he has just established the spirit and presence of God. Again, Trevor pauses to measure his words. Finally, he looks up again and says, "I continue to feel responsible for Hal's death. I cannot forgive myself. I need to hear from you."

I ask, "Tell God what you need to hear?"

"I need to know in my heart that you forgive me. Although I know you do not condemn me, I still feel this terrible guilt. It is very important that I hear your forgiveness."

I say, "Reverse roles."

In the role of God, Trevor says, "You already know that Hal's death was the result of an accident. You also know you reacted in the moment the best way you could. You feel guilty because it is your way of staying close to Hal. Absolving yourself does not mean you forget Hal. You don't need my forgiveness because there is no guilt."

I am not surprised by the insight shown by Trevor because he has given much thought to this encounter. I simply need to place him in the role of the ultimate authority as he views his world. From that position, he has little option but to gather the truth as he sees it.

It is always possible, however, that the outcome may be less positive. It is important that the therapist have patience and find the path of constructive growth. Listen carefully to how the session unfolds. Patiently listen to the client and anticipate ways for the client to experience a positive resolution. If, for example, a reproachful statement comes from God, continued role reversals with God will help the client explore the origin of the feeling and find a resolution to the dilemma.

After Trevor finishes his role as God, I ask him to reverse roles to further validate what has been said. I say, "Tell me how this has helped you?" (*Sharing phase.*)

"I guess I have always known that I am hanging on to the guilt fearing I will forget Hal and what he means to me. I know I won't forget him. I think I have tried too hard to hang on to him. I need to let go. I know he would tell me to let go if he were here. I need to convince myself that letting go *means I can still hold his memory close* even if or when I form new relationships. I've been told life is for the living. I think I finally understand that."

I ask, "Trevor, are you satisfied that you accomplished what you came for?"

"I think so because I am looking at the whole experience differently. If I slip back, I know I can call you again."

I end the session by assuring him that he accomplished a great deal by working hard each session. I also assure him that I am available when he needs me. He leaves my office with what seems to be a more determined expression than when he first came to see me.

Dr. John Nolte is my mentor and happened to direct my first psychodrama during my training. With John, I began my journey with psychodrama by dealing with leftover anger about the loss of my left arm at the age of five. It was John who gently went with me to that mountaintop on a Colorado ski lift where I communed with God to find answers. I strongly recommend Nolte's article in which he underscores the need to psychodramatically help protagonists find the supernatural being in their lives when it becomes evident that it will help find closure. John (1975) writes, "It is fitting that psychodrama provides a client a concrete means of accomplishing the feat of getting in touch with one's 'I-God.'"

I am reminded that I must continue to find ways for clients to actively engage in their search for answers and then get out of the way.

Chapter Thirteen

CONCLUSIONS

What lessons come from this sampling of cases? What makes action-oriented counseling unique? What sets it apart from traditional talk-listen counseling?

First, action-oriented therapy is existential. Issues are brought into the moment. This aspect of psychodrama embodies the power of the method. Following adequate warm-up, we can relive a moment in time that may have had profound influence on our life. Revisiting an experience from another time and space brings it into the present moment. A new reality (a new conserve) is created around the event, and we see with new eyes and feel with new hands. We experience surplus reality because we have spontaneously created it. Blomkvist, Moreno, and Rutzel (2000) say that surplus reality is one of the most vital, curative, and mysterious elements of psychodrama.

The new view casts a new light that illuminates new perceptions and new understandings of life that have been conserved for years in an unyielding shape. The cultural conserve is fractured by the reality of new perceptions. Our view of personal history will never be the same. Change has resulted from stepping over the picture frame, into the painting, and exploring life within the third dimension.

Second, psychodrama requires a specific way of thinking. The therapist must shift from a traditional spoken conversational mode to an action mode. The counselor can easily revert to questions and answers that can derail the client from an action-focused session to a conventional talk-listen-oriented session. From the moment the warm-up phase begins, the psychodramatically oriented counselor looks for a clue that will open the door to action. Unless a counselor deliberately creates ways for the client to dramatize his or her exploration, it is easy to say, "Tell me," rather than, "Show me."

The point is this. The action-oriented counselor believes that change occurs more quickly and more effectively when a client steps into the third dimension of his or her life. There is no other method that enables a client to experience a new reality (surplus reality) from which perceptions can be created that frees the client to look back and look forward with a unique vision.

The action-oriented counselor does not abandon neither his or her knowledge of human behavior nor the competence to formulate diagnostic conclusions. The counselor avoids lengthy dialogue with the client and replaces it with action that leads the client through experiences that open new windows through which the client views life. The counselor becomes a director of action from which the client learns and gains new insights that lead to further action. Eventually the client claims ownership of discoveries and adds a new page to his or her choices—new conserves.

Third, the boundary that separates client from counselor is consistently observed. The counselor often is enticed to join in the drama by doubling for the client or assuming the role of an absent person. Resist this. The counselor must remain the firm anchor that maintains a positive flow of action. When a counselor crosses the boundary, the client has the additional burden of keeping separate the counselor as counselor and the counselor as auxiliary.

The probability of transference increases when the counselor becomes a part of the drama. The client who identifies the counselor as an auxiliary in the drama can experience difficulty returning him or her to the role of counselor. Of course, there is always the problem of countertransference creating ideations and behaviors counterproductive to counseling.

Fourth, the counselor gives autonomy to the client. That means the client owns the insights, discoveries, and conclusions that emerge from the action and interactions. Change of perceptions come from experiencing portions of life needing examination, not from a counselor who shares his or her discoveries and proceeds to convince the client to take a new direction.

Fifth, remember essential methods of psychodrama. The warm-up gives you an idea where to begin action. Action moves the client along pathways that lead to discoveries. Action involves role reversal, role training, doubling, multiple doubling, empty chairs, mirror work, catharsis, surplus reality, soliloquy, scene setting, intrapsychic and interpsychic encounter, concretization, role training, and, of course, director and protagonist. You will find many more terms in the literature.

Remember, when you are interviewing an absent person, it is best to move from the periphery to the center—from the least to the more intrusive questions. Also let the protagonist answer his or her own questions, and never stop the action with the protagonist in the absent person's role.

Finally, and perhaps most important, the counselor must make the transition from talking to the client about the dilemma to creating a way for the client to dramatize the dilemma, and put issues into action. My years in directing psychodrama and the nearly two decades of teaching psychodrama to graduate students taught me that making the change from traditional counseling to action-oriented dramatization is very difficult.

As I have said before, action-focused therapy frequently is the method of choice. I am not advocating that other methods are inappropriate or ineffective. My objective is to place another therapeutic method at a counselor's disposal. I use the term *method* rather than *technique* because psychodrama is much more than a mere set of techniques.

I do not believe that it is helpful to take my car to a mechanic who lifts the hood and begins pushing, pulling, and banging at everything with his screwdriver. I ask, "Why are you only using a screwdriver?" He answers, "I am a screwdriver mechanic." Our profession needs no "screwdriver counselors." We need counselors familiar with many therapeutic tools. Psychodrama is one more tool.

Finally, I recommend a firm grounding in the methods of psychodrama. Attendance in at least four or five psychodrama workshops will greatly enhance your understanding and skill. Also, this method often provokes strong emotional responses from clients. Practitioners need to be comfortable reacting appropriately to these emotions with respect and gentleness. Also, psychodrama clinicians require several hundred hours of supervised special training in group dynamics and managing group interaction. Therefore, this book will not qualify you as a psychodramatist. My objective is to add action methods to individual counseling and pique your interest to get further training in psychodrama. This book belongs in the counseling toolbox.

REFERENCE LIST

Berne, Eric (1947) *The Mind in Action*, Simon and Schuster, New York, NY.

Berne, Eric (1961) *Transactional Analysis in Psychotherapy*, Grove Press, New York, NY.

Berne, Eric (1964) *Games People Play*, Grove Press, New York, NY.

Blomkvist, Dag, Moreno, Zerka T., and Rutzel, Thomas (2000) *Psychodrama, Surplus Reality and the Art of Healing*, Routledge, New York, NY.

Brill, A. A. 1995 (Ed.) *The Basic Writings of Sigmund Freud*, The Modern Library, New York, NY.

Buchanan, D. R., and Garcia A., (2008) *Psychodrama in Individual Therapy: Psychodrama A Deux*, Retrieved September 16, 2008 from http://www.psychodramatraining.com/article1.htm

Casson, John (1997) *Psychodrama in Individual Psychotherapy*, Journal of British Psychodrama and Sociometry, Vol. 12

Coopersmith, S (1967) *The Antecedents of Self-Esteem*, W. H. Freeman and Company, San Francisco, CA.

Corey, Gerald (1996) *Theory and Practice of Counseling and Psychotherapy*, Brooks and Cole, Pacific Grove, CA.

Corey, Gerald (2000) *Theory and Practice of Counseling and Psychotherapy*. 6th ed. Wadsworth and Thomson Learning, and Thomson Learning, CA.

Cukier, Rosa (2008) *Bipersonal Psychodrama: Its Techniques, Therapists, and Clients.* Lulu.com.

Daytron, Tian (1994) *The Drama Within, Psychodrama and Experiential Therapy,* Health Communications, Inc., Deerfield Beach, FL.

De Shazer, S., Dolan, Y., with Korman H., Trepper, T. S., McCollan, E., Berg, I. K. (2007) *More than Miracles: The State of the Art of Solution-focused Brief Therapy,* Hawworth Press, Binghamton, N.Y.

Dreikurs, R & Grey, L. (1968) *Logical Consequences: A New Approach Discipline,* Meredith Press, New York, NY.

Ellis, Albert, (2001) *Overcoming Destructive Beliefs, Feelings, and Behaviors, New Directions for Rational Emotive Behavior Therapy,* Prometheus Books.

Erikson, Erik, (1950) *Childhood and Society,* Norton, New York:

Frankl, Victor, (1963) *Man's Search for Meaning,* Pocket Books, New York.

Freud, S. (1901) *The Psychopathology of Everyday Life,* Vol. 6 of *The Standard Edition of the Complete Psychological Works of Sigmund Freud,* Hogarth, London, England.

Gladding, S. (1996) *Counseling: A Comprehensive Profession* (3rd ed.), Prentice Hall, N.J.

Glasser, William, (1984) *Control Theory,* Harper and Row, New York, NY.

Glasser, William, (1965) *Reality Therapy,* Harper and Row, New York, NY.

Glasser, William, (1986) *Control Theory in the Classroom,* Harper and Row, New York, NY.

Gilbert, D. & Buckner, R. (2007, January) Time Travel in the Brain, *Time,* New York, NY.

Goldman E. E. & Morrison, D. S. (1984), *Psychodrama: Experience and Process,* Kendall/Hunt, Dubuque, IA.

Goldstein, L. A. (1971) Investigation of Doubling as a Technique for Involving Severely Withdrawn Patients in Group Psychotherapy, *Journal of Consulting & Clinical Psychotherapy*, Vol. 37, pp. 155-162.

Harris, J. B. (2002) *Gestalt Therapy in Groups: The Early Days*, Manchester Gestalt Centre, Manchester, England.

Harris, T. A. (1969) *I'm OK—You're OK, A Practical Guide to Transactional Analysis*, Harper, Row, New York, NY.

Jennings, S. (1992) *Drama Therapy: Theory and Practice*, Travistock/Routledge, London, England.

Jung, C. G. (1934) The Archetypes and the Collective Unconscious, found in (1968) *Collected Works of C. G. Jung*, Vol. 9, Part 1, 2nd ed. Princeton University Press, Princeton, N.J.

Kipper, D (1986) *Psychotherapy Through Role Playing*, Brunner/Mazel, NY.

Knittel, Marvin G., (2007) Hanging On and Letting Go: The Parents' Dilemma, in *Counseling Today*, an American Counseling Association Publication, March.

Kantrowitz, Barbara, Tyre, Peg, (2006) *The Fine Art of Letting Go*, Newsweek, May 22.

Kubler-Ross, Elisabeth, (1969) *On Death and Dying*, MacMillan Publishing Co., New York, NY.

Latner, Joel, (1992) *The Theory of Gestalt Therapy, Gestalt Therapy: Perspectives and Applications*, Edwin Nevis (ed.) Gestalt Press, Cambridge, MA

Landy, R. (1992) *One-on-One, The Role of the Dramatherapist Working with Individuals*, Chapter 7 (pp. 98-111) in Jennings, S. book *Dramatherapy, Theory, and Practice*, Travistock/Routledge, London, England.

Marineau, R. (1989) *Jacob Levy Moreno 1889-1974: Father of Psychodrama, Sociometry and Group Psychotherapy*, Travistock/Routledge, London and New York.

Moreno J. L. (1947) *The Future of Man's World*, Psychodrama Monographs, Beacon House, New York, NY.

Moreno J. L. (1953) *Who Shall Survive?* Foundations of Sociometry, Group Psychotherapy and Psychodrama, Beacon House Inc., Beacon, N.Y.

Moreno, J. L. (1966) Psychiatry of the Twentieth Century: Function of the Universal: Time, Space, Reality, and Cosmos, *Psychodrama, Vol. 3*, pp. 11-23. In Fox, Jonathan (Ed.) The Essential Moreno, p. 3, Springer, New York, NY.

Moreno J. L. (1973) Notes on Indications and Contra-indications for Acting Out in Psychodrama, *Group Psychotherapy Psychodrama & Sociometry*, Vol. 26.

Moreno, J. L. in collaboration with Z. T. Moreno (1975) *Psychodrama: Foundations of Psychotherapy*, Vol. 2, Beacon House, New York, NY.

Moreno, J. L. *Psychodrama, Vol. 1, 4th edition*, Beacon House, Inc, Beacon, New York, NY.

Moreno J. L., (1985) (copyright Zerka T. Moreno & Jonathan D. Moreno) *The Autobiography of J. L. Moreno, M.D.*, (Abridged). Moreno Institute East, Archives, Harvard University.

Moreno, J. L. (1989) *The Autobiography of J. L. Moreno*, MD, (Ed.) Jonathan D. Moreno, Journal of Group Psychotherapy, Psychodrama, & Sociometry, Vol.42, No. 1 and 2, Spring and Summer, Heldref Publications, Washington, DC.

Moreno, Z., Blomkvisty, D., Rutzel, T., 2000 *Psychodrama: Surplus Reality and the Art of Healing*, Routledge, New York, NY.

Moreno, Zerka (1982) *Psychodramatic Rules, Techniques and Adjunctive Methods, Psychodrama and Group Psychotherapy Monograph*, No. 41, Beacon House, Inc., Horsham Foundation, Ambler, PA.

Nolte, John, (2008) *The Psychodrama Papers*, Encounter Publications, 97 Cumberland Street, Hartford, CT.

Nolte, John, Smallwood, Cynthia, & Weistart, James (1975) *Role Reversal with God*, Group Psychotherapy, & Psychodrama, 28, 70-76.

Penfield, W. (1952) Memory Mechanism, *Archives of Neurology and Psychiatry*, Vol. 67, AMA, Washington, DC.

Perls, F., Hefferline, R., & Goldman, P. (1951) *Gestalt Therapy: Excitement and Growth in Human Personality*, Julian, New York, NY.

Perls, F. (1973) *The Gestalt Approach and Eyewitness to Therapy*, California Science and Behavior Books, Palo Alto, CA, in Bantam Books, (1976) New York, NY.

Ramsey, A., Watson, P., Biderman, M., Reeves, A. (1996) Self Reported Narcissism and Perceived Parental Permissiveness and Authoritarianism, *Journal of Genetic Psychology*, Vol. 157, No. 2.

Rogers, Carl (1942) *Newer Concepts in Practice, Counseling and Psychotherapy*, Houghton Mifflin, Boston, MA.

Rogers, Carl (1951) *Client-Centered Therapy: Its Current Practice, Implication, and Theory*, Houghton Mifflin, Boston, MA.

Rogers, Carl (1961) *On Becoming a Person*, Houghton Mifflin Company, Boston, MA.

Rogers, Carl (1978) *On Personal Power*, Dell Publishing, New York, NY.

Shapiro, F. (2001) *Eye Movement Desensitization and Reprocessing*, (2nd Ed.) Guilford Press, New York, NY.

Stein, Marsha B., Callahan, Monica L. (1982) *The Use of Psychodrama in Individual Psychotherapy*, Journal of Group Psychotherapy, Psychodrama, & Sociometry, 35, 118-129. Washington D.C., Helderf Publications.

Tobin, Stephin, *Gestalt Therapy*, **Retrieved October 26, 2008 from http:// www.doctortobin.Com/pages/perls.shtml.**

Vander May, James (1980) Unpublished paper produced on website by Adam Blatner, May, 2008, **Retrieved November 2, 2008, from http:// www. blatner.com/ Adam/pdutbk/vandrmyadeux.html**

Welter, Paul R. (1987) *Counseling and the Search for Meaning*, Word Books, Waco, Texas.

Welter, Paul R. (1990) *How to Help A Friend.* (Revised Edition), Tyndale House Publishers, Inc., Wheaton, Ill.

White, M. & Epson, D. (1990) *Narrative Means to Therapeutic Ends, W.W.* Norton, New York, NY.

Yalom, V. (2004) An Interview with Zerka Moreno, TEP, *Psychotherapy. net: resources To inspire therapists,* **Retrieved December 12, 2008, from http://www.psychotherapy.net/interview/Zerka_Moreno.**

INDEX

A

action phase methods, types of
  intrapsychic and interpsychic
    encounter, 95
  role training, 95
Alice (Joyce's daughter), 60–65, 103
Angie, 74–82, 103
Anna O., 22, 103
Antecedents of Self-Esteem (Coopersmith),
  74

B

Becky (Joyce's daughter), 60–65, 103
Berg, I. K., 26, 103
Berne, Eric, 25
*Bipersonal Psychodrama: Its Techniques,
    Therapists, and Clients* (Cukier), 30
Blomkvist, 94, 103
Breuer, 22, 103
Buchanan, Dale, 29–31

C

Callahan, Monica, 28–30
case studies
  on aging, 83–86, 103
  on being more assertive, 32–35, 104
  on dealing with parent-child
    disengaging, 45, 59–65, 104
  on dealing with "unfinished" business,
    47–49, 104
  on dealing with unresolved guilt,
    87–92, 106
  on dependency, 66–73, 104
  on depression, 50–58
  on discovering meaning, 32–35
  on sexual abuse, 36–46, 104
Casson, John, 28–31
catharsis, 22–23, 28, 41, 49, 85, 89, 95,
  103
  of abreaction, 22, 25, 28, 44–45, 103
  of integration, 23, 28, 85
cathartic therapy, 22. *See also* catharsis
Chuck (depressed client), 50–58
Clara (client having difficulty handling
    aging), 83–86
coaching, 17

concretization, 27, 31, 95, 103
conserve, 21–23, 25, 41, 53, 94
  cultural, 21–23, 94
Coopersmith, Stanley, 74
  Antecedents of Self-Esteem, 74, 103–4
counseling, 17–18, 20, 24–27, 31, 36–39,
    41, 45, 66, 68, 75, 95–96
  action-oriented, 24, 94
  client-centered, 27
  solution-focused, 26–27
Cukier, Rosa, 29–31
  Bipersonal Psychodrama: Its Techniques,
    Therapists, and Clients, 30

D

Dayton, Tian, 24
de Shazer, S., 26
doubling, 27, 30–31, 44, 55, 58, 66, 95
dramatherapy, 24, 28–29

E

ego state
  adult, 25
  child, 25
  parent, 25
Ellis, Albert, 25
Emily (sexual abuse victim), 36, 38–46
Epston, David, 25
  Narrative Means to Therapeutic Ends, 25
Eric (Chuck's brother), 54–56, 58
experiential situation, methods of
  empty-chair, 23–24, 27, 31, 95
  enactment and dramatization, 23
  guided fantasy, 23–24, 104
  monodrama, 23–24, 104
  self-dialogue, 23–24, 104

F

Frankl, Viktor, 26
Freud, Sigmund, 19, 22

G

Gall, Joseph, 17
Garcia, Antonina, 29–31
George (client struggling with being
  assertive), 32–35
Gilbert, Daniel, 29
Glasser, William, 20, 22, 51, 53
Grace (Grant's mother), 69, 104
Grant (client with dependency issues),
  66–73
guided imagery, 27, 29, 55

H

Hal (Trevor's life partner), 87–90, 92,
  104
Harold (Joe's father), 48–49
Harris, T. A.
  I'm OK—You're OK, 25

I

I'm OK—You're OK (Harris), 25

J

Joe (client struggling with his father's
  death), 47–49
John (Emily's father), 43–45
Joyce (client struggling with parent-child
  disengaging), 45, 59–65
Jung, Carl, 83

K

Kantrowitz, Barbara, 59
Kipper, David, 28–30
  Psychotherapy Through Role Playing, 28
Kubler-Ross, Elisabeth, 47

L

Landy, Robert, 29–30
logotherapy, 26, 105

M

Martinez, Alonzo, 74–82, 105
Martinez, Angelica. *See* Angie
Martinez, Juanita, 74–82, 105
Moreno, J. L., 18–23, 26–28, 30–31,
    85–86
Moreno, Zerka, 19, 23–25, 30, 94

N

Narrative Means to Therapeutic Ends
    (Epston and White), 25
Nolte, John, 20, 93

P

Parsons, Frank, 17
Penfield, Wilder, 18
Perls, Fritz, 21, 23–24
phrenology, 17
psychoanalysis, 17, 22, 30, 105
psychodrama, 17–21, 23–31, 35, 46, 48,
    65, 74, 82, 85–86, 90, 93–96
  bipersonal, 30
  phases of
    action, 21, 25–26, 28–29, 31–33, 38,
      46, 50, 75, 86, 89–91, 94–96
    sharing, 26, 28, 34, 37, 41, 49, 64, 68,
      72, 83, 92
    warm-up, 26, 28, 37–38, 41, 48,
      50, 53–54, 57, 61, 67, 75, 87, 90,
      94–95, 105
  techniques for
    auxiliary chair, 29, 105
    dream reenactment, 30, 105
    empty-chair, 23–24, 27, 31, 95

future projection, 29
high chair, 30, 56–57
magic shop, 30, 105
metaphors, 30, 51
mirroring, 27, 29, 31, 58, 95, 105
multiple doubling, 27, 31, 95
myths, 30, 105
scene setting, 27, 29–30, 42, 95, 105
soliloquy, 27, 29, 36, 41, 45, 88, 95,
    105
See also dramatherapy
psychodrama à deux, 26–31, 36
psychodramatic roles
  audience, 24, 27
  auxiliary egos, 24, 27, 29–30, 105
  director, 21, 24, 26–30, 34–35, 44–45,
    91, 95
  double, 24, 27, 29, 43–45, 55, 59, 70
  protagonist, 21, 23–24, 26–28, 46, 93,
    95, 105
Psychotherapy Through Role Playing
    (Kipper), 28

R

rational emotive behavior therapy, 25, 27
Rogers, Carl, 17, 26
Rutzel, T., 94

S

Sam (Joyce's husband), 59–65, 105
spontaneity, 20–23, 27, 39, 86
spontaneity-creativity, 20–21, 23, 25–26,
    28, 31, 85, 105
Stein, Marcia, 28–30
surplus reality, 18, 22–24, 26, 28, 31–32,
    39, 54, 94–95
  techniques for
    role reversal, 24, 26–29, 31–32, 41,
      47–48, 50, 58–59, 62, 66, 74–75,
      82, 86–87, 90, 92

T

tele, 21, 26–27, 40, 106
therapy, types of
　art, 24
　cognitive-behavioral, 20
　dance, 24
　expressive, 24
　Gestalt, 21, 23–24, 27, 48
　holding, 24
　narrative, 25
　play, 24
　primal, 24
　reality, 20, 22, 27, 53
　solution-focused, 26
　T-groups, 24, 106
Tobin, Stephan, 21
Tom (Emily's husband), 37–42, 44, 46, 106
transactional analysis, 25

Trevor (client struggling with life partner's death), 87–92
Tyre, Peg, 59

V

Vander May, James, 29–30

W

Walters, Rebecca, 31
White, Michael, 25
　Narrative Means to Therapeutic Ends, 25
wisdom figure, 30, 49, 74, 79–80, 82, 106

Y

Yalom, Victor, 19, 23